Renard.

# IGNORANCE, FAITH AND CONFORMITY

# IGNORANCE, FAITH AND CONFORMITY

## STUDIES IN MORAL THEOLOGY

BY

## KENNETH E. KIRK

FELLOW OF TRINITY COLLEGE, AND FORMERLY
FELLOW OF MAGDALEN COLLEGE, OXFORD;
SIX-PREACHER IN CANTERBURY CATHEDRAL

LONGMANS, GREEN AND CO.

39 PATERNOSTER ROW, LONDON, E.C.4.

NEW YORK, TORONTO
BOMBAY, CALCUTTA AND MADRAS

1925

# PREFACE

THE following chapters may be said to have a triple purpose.

1. Just as the formulated doctrines of Christianity cannot fully be understood without a knowledge of the history which underlies each several article and phrase, so it is impossible to reach an intelligent apprehension of the moral theology of the Schoolmen or of post-Reformation Catholicism without a similar knowledge of the causes which led to the formulation of their important terms and distinctions. The present book is concerned in the first instance with one such term, ' invincible ignorance ' ; and some of the more important phases of its history are noticed in chapters I and II. In chapter IV a similar attempt has been made in respect of a single point of history —the scope and significance of St. Thomas' discussion of faith ; and if the result is to correct in some measure the inadequate account of his teaching on this subject given in an earlier book (' Some Principles of Moral Theology,' chap. iv.), the labour involved will have been worth while.

2. ' Invincible ignorance ' is however the connecting theme of the book, and the subject was not chosen haphazard. As is suggested in the first paragraph of chapter I, the history of moral theology is, in one important aspect, the history of the Church's unceasing attempt to adjust an ' infallible rule ' to the demands of the individual conscience. But if, when all possible adjustments have been made, the question still arises (as it has arisen in all ages), ' Can there *now* be any excuse for the individual if he acts contrary

to the law ? ' it must be faced.   It is well to set out from
τὰ ὁμολογούμενα, as Aristotle suggests ;  and there is only
one case in which theologians and philosophers are all
agreed that violation of the law is no sin.   That case is of
the kind known as ' invincible ignorance.'   I have therefore
started at this point and attempted to consider how far
the admission has carried the Church to a recognition of individual liberties in the face of promulgated law, and how
much further it might carry her.   Chapters II and III and
the end of chapter IV are devoted to this enquiry, which
naturally enough overlaps with the one previously indicated.

3. English Churchmen as a whole are agreed (subject
to minor and individual reservations) that the Anglican
system offers a field for the reconciliation of law and liberty
at least as hopeful as that of any other communion.   Of
recent writers, Bishop Gore ('The Holy Spirit and the Church,'
chap. XI) has vindicated Anglicanism, in this respect, from
the point of view of fidelity to the teaching of Our Lord
and the practice of the primitive community ;  Mr. Rawlinson
(' Authority and Freedom ') has done the same from the
point of view of right reason and the needs of the religious
personality.   The final chapter of this book approaches the
same subject from another angle—one which, if not so important as those just mentioned, is not without weight in the
minds of many who are exercised with the matter.   To them
the problem presents itself, ' Does the Anglican system fall
within the limits of a legitimate development of the principles
of Western Christendom as a whole ?   Does it incorporate,
or does it ignore, the best experience of fifteen centuries of
Catholicism in the matter of authority and the individual? '
There would appear to be no way of answering this question
except by an examination of the principles of moral theology
and canon law in the West.   In chapter V therefore it is
suggested (after a survey admittedly too brief for the
importance of the question) that the Anglican emphasis

upon custom, as contrasted with positive law, will stand the test of these principles ; and that the liberty of thought and conscience allowed in our system is no more than a working example of the doctrine of invincible ignorance in a new, but in no way non-Catholic, environment.

Readers to whom the exact definition and close argument which characterised scholasticism are uncongenial, or to whom it appears as a method of exposition and enquiry unsuited to so sacred a matter as religion, will find this book both idle and unnecessary. Nor would they be moved very much by the consideration that all modern formularies, those of the Protestant reformers no less than those of Anglicanism and Rome, look back to the Schoolmen as the source of their terminology and categories. Where this is the case, it can only be suggested that some little interest may be derived from the history of a development whose most striking characteristic is that, not once but several times in the process, humanity and Christian charity are to be seen making new demands upon an apparently closed system, and triumphantly forcing it to comply by an enlargement of its scope.

The material here presented is drawn in the main from the original sources ; but chapter III owes some of its references to Fr. S. Harent's exhaustive article on ' Infidèles ' in Vacant and Mangenot's still incomplete ' Dictionnaire de la Théologie Catholique.' Especially is this the case with Tritheim and Seyssel, with whom I should otherwise have remained unacquainted ; but the originality of their point of view has led me to give them more extended notice than they have received from Fr. Harent. To the same article, as also to Cardinal Billot's unfinished series on ' La Providence de Dieu ' in ' Études,' I owe a great deal of general enlightenment on the question treated in that chapter. Other obligations are, I hope, sufficiently acknowledged where they occur.

Of a different and far more important character is my debt
to the Rev. C. J. Shebbeare, Rector of Stanhope and Wilde
Lecturer in Natural and Comparative Religion in the University of Oxford, who read the entire book in manuscript and
subjected it to detailed and exhaustive criticism. Many
of his most valuable suggestions I have incorporated in
the text; some, though commanding my entire agreement,
were of so distinctive a kind that I felt myself incompetent
to deal with them. Particularly is this the case wherever
the subject-matter touches upon the deeper philosophical
problems underlying the questions both of ignorance and
of obligation. At these points the need for further treatment is, as Mr. Shebbeare pointed out, very obvious indeed ;
its absence must be put down not to any failure on
the part of the critic, but to the equally obvious limitations
of the writer. But my gratitude to Mr. Shebbeare is no
less intense because I have been unable to rise to the
standard he required of me, and I take this opportunity
of giving it expression. Dr. Darwell Stone and Canon
Lacey, with equal kindness, read and criticised the last
chapter, as well as some other parts of the book ; and I have
gratefully incorporated their suggestions. The irksome task
of reading the proofs was discharged by the Rev. E. H. Ward,
Lecturer in Ecclesiastical History in the University of
Sheffield, and the Rev. E. Graham, Fellow of Oriel College,
Oxford ; to them also my warmest thanks are due.

OXFORD,
     *November* 1924.

# CONTENTS

# IGNORANCE, FAITH AND CONFORMITY

## CHAPTER I

### IGNORANCE

### I

THE history of moral theology in the West is in the main a history of successive attempts to adjust the claims of conscience to the claims of law. On the one hand, the Church inherited, from her Jewish forefathers, an unbounded respect for the Mosaic dispensation and the will of God as revealed in the prophets ; and was happily enabled, by means of the allegorical method of interpretation, to regard the greater part of the Old Testament as enshrining a divine code in no way at variance with the New. She took over, furthermore, from Greek philosophers and Roman lawyers, a respect scarcely less unbounded for the ' law of nature ' [1]

On the ' law of nature ' see particularly Maine, *Ancient Law*, c. 3 ; E. Zeller, ' Über Begriff und Begrundung der Sittlichen Gesetze ' (in *Abhandlungen der Akademie der Wissenschaften zu Berlin*, 1882) ; F. C. French, ' Concept of Law in Ethics ' (*Philosophical Review*, vol. ii., 1893). The idea of a law, distinguished from *human* law because unwritten and universal, and (less clearly) from *positive divine* law because ' man cannot point to the time and place of its promulgation,' goes back a long way (see especially Soph., *Antig.*, 450 ff. ; *Œd. Rex*, 465, 864 ; Thuc., ii. 37), and is earlier than the idea of ' laws of nature ' as applied to the principles of the cosmic order. The Stoics both strengthened the concept of the ' natural moral law,' and developed from it that of the ' cosmic laws of nature ' ; the

—a code implanted in primeval man even before the age of revelation, and still promulgating itself in the consciousness of every child as he came to maturity. With a confidence as touching as it was unfounded, she held that the 'first principles' of the law of nature were indefectible in every man,[1] and could be enunciated with unfailing accuracy;[2] and the belief lasted on even though scepticism denied the possibility of proving that some of the most widely recognised of these 'principles' belonged to the law of nature at all. This was her double inheritance; but her own experience at once confirmed and enriched it. To the teaching of the incarnate Son of God as recorded in the gospel the Christian could extend nothing but an unquestioning and grateful acceptance; the writings of those who had first received His revelation commanded an almost equal respect. The assistance of the Holy Spirit promised and given to the Church involved the conviction that where the Christian community added to the corpus of natural and revealed law by later enactments as to faith and morals, its definitions must be in line with what had gone before—

Roman lawyers drew upon their experience of the common element in the different 'laws of nations' to give it a positive content. Christianity could perfectly well have discarded the 'law of nature,' or allowed it to remain as a shadowy original now superseded by the 'positive revealed law'; but it refused to do so, and the result was remarkable. The 'law of nature' remained as a potential weapon in the armoury of every controversialist. As the Stoics used it to detach men from the narrow bounds of the city state, so Abailard used it against traditionalism (see the *Dialogue*), Gerson against the papacy, Hobbes against republicanism, the Jesuits against the civil power; whilst the part played by the conception in the French and American revolutions is well known. See further, p. 37.

[1] Tert., *de an.*, 41: 'quod enim a Deo est non tam extinguitur quam obumbratur. Potest enim obumbrari quia non est Deus; extingui non potest quia a Deo est'; Aug., *Conf.*, ii. 4: 'lex scripta in cordibus hominum, quam ne ipsa quidem delet iniquitas'; other patristic references in Koch-Preuss, *Handbook of Moral Theology*, i, pp. 122–124. Cp. Aquinas, *S.T.*, i. 2, q. 91, a. 2; q. 94, a. 6; and 'dictum Gratiani' in *Corp. Jur. Can.*, c. 12, C. I, q. 4: '<ignorantia> naturalis <juris> omnibus adultis damnabilis'; and commonly.

[2] *S.T.*, i. 2, q. 94, aa. 3, 4.

they were not additions to, but rather developments and articulations of, the original deposit.[1]

The respect thus offered to law in various directions was therefore all concentrated in practice upon the Church, which had inherited the old dispensation, recognised the natural moral law, been founded under the auspices of the new code, and become the final and only vehicle of this manifold revelation to men. Theologically this took shape in a conception of the infallibility, or at least the indefectibility, of the Church. This conception for the moment we shall have sufficiently explored if we explain it as meaning, in practice, that the official pronouncements of the Church had a binding and authoritative claim to obedience; whilst her unofficial pronouncements, or the dicta of theologians which she had tacitly endorsed, had a strong though not absolutely compelling authority of the same kind.[2] At first sight such a system would seem to leave little room for individual liberty, except in those corners and crannies of belief and behaviour upon which the law had not laid its tentacles; and it speaks volumes for the genius of Christendom that, side by side with this intense recognition of the claims of law, it extended an equal recognition to the claims of conscience.

There was, however, that in the consciousness of individual Christians which refused to be bound by law. Union with Christ produced a conviction of immediate personal guidance from Him; the assistance of the Spirit was felt by individual believers as intensely as by the corporate body. This inherent and universally admitted tendency to act along the lines of individual liberty was recognised as a wholly Christian thing; and to it the

[1] So *S.T.*, ii. 2, q. 1, a. 7: 'quaecumque posteriores crediderunt, continebantur in fide praecedentium patrum, licet implicite.' Cp. Suarez, *de fid. theol.*, ii. 6; de Lugo, *de virt. fid. div.*, iii. 5. Similarly on conduct, *S.T.*, i. 2, q. 91, a. 3.

[2] See further, *infra*, p. 143.

name of 'conscience,'[1] as the 'internal norm' of action,
was given. To this recognition of conscience by the side
of law, and to the inevitable conflict which resulted from it,
is due much of the internal history of Christendom ; to it
also are due most of the perplexing technical terms and
distinctions of formulated moral theology.

Thus the attempt to mitigate the rigour of law to the
weak or tender conscience produced, or at all events
developed, the distinctions between counsel and precept,
between mortal and venial sin, between contrition and
attrition. On the other hand the desire to emancipate
the individual Christian from the vexatious interference
of merely detailed formalism was responsible, in part at
least, for the various attempts at casuistry which culminated
in probabilism. With neither of these developments are
we here concerned, for they do not touch the heart of the
problem. A point must come when even under the most
genial and paternal system of law all possible mitigations
and relaxations have been exhausted. What is to happen
then ? The question will at length arise, Can any further

---

[1] A history of the development of the idea of conscience in the early
Church, along the lines of J. Jahnel's sketch (de conscientiae notione,
Berlin, 1862), is urgently needed. The judicial aspect of conscience is
recognised even in the most primitive forms of religion and ethics ; its
preceptive authority for the individual comes later. There are anticipations of it in the Greek tragedians, but the idea first appears in full view
with the Stoics. It was their special doctrine of morality as a life according to nature which appears to have determined the name (συνείδησις,
'conscientia') given to the hitherto nameless conception ; for to live in
accordance with nature you must first have consciousness or cognition of
the law of nature both around and within yourself. In Christianity, the
East appears early to have connected the idea of conscience as a guide
with that of communion with God and the voice of the Holy Spirit ;
Clement (Strom., ii. 6) speaks of ἡ θεόθεν ἤκουσα συνείδησις, which gives δύναμις
κυριακὴ (vi. 14) ; Origen (ad Rom., ii. 15) identifies it with the Spirit. In
the West the recognition of conscience as the internal monitor owes a good
deal to the Pelagians (Jahnel, 67), who laid stress upon its purity in opposition to exaggerated doctrines of original sin. Abailard, in the Scito
Teipsum, makes it the final test of right action ; and it was perhaps the
importance which he attached to it which stimulated the Schoolmen to
give the subject particular attention.

liberty be allowed to the individual, or must he in the end conform, on pain of exclusion from the society and from the promise of benefits which its membership conveys? Is there any case whatever (beyond those contemplated in the distinctions just mentioned) in which the Christian can conscientiously act in violation of the laws promulgated by the Church to which he belongs, and yet remain a loyal member of the Church, recognised as such by his fellows?

Common sense at once suggests an answer. Where a law is broken through sheer ignorance either of its existence or of its applicability in a given case, there seems a likelihood that the offender is free from guilt. ' Ignorantia juris nulla excusatio,' is no doubt a principle of civil law; [1] but the Church as a spiritual society is dealing not with civil offences but with moral culpability. There were indeed those who, following some at least of St. Augustine's clues,[2] applied the principle of the 'Digest' to questions of faith and morals, and asserted that ignorance of the Christian moral law even on the part of the unevangelised heathen, as itself sharing the guilt of original sin, could afford no excuse for breaches of that law. This theory, however, was no more than an à priori deduction from the general principle that original sin involved some kind of individual guilt in the posterity of Adam; and the Church in general

[1] *Digest*, xxii. 9. 6.

[2] Thus *de grat. et lib. arb.*, c. 3 (5) : ' Even the ignorance (not of those who refuse to learn knowledge, but) of those who are, as it were, simply ignorant, does not so far excuse a man as to exempt him from the penalty of eternal fire, even if his failure to believe has been the result of his not having heard at all what it is he should believe; though probably his punishment may be a milder one.' Cp. *Ep.* 194, 6 (27) : ' inexcusabilis est omnis peccator . . . sive qui novit sive qui ignorat '; so, too, *de corr. et grat.*, 7 (12). Augustine acted upon the same principle, confessing, as Jeremy Taylor says, ' the sins of his first years, the peevishness of his infancy, his wrangling with his nurses, his very envying for the nurse's milk and fond names '; to which Taylor adds the comment : ' This was indeed a greater piety than reason ' (*Duct. Dub.*, iv. 1, rule vi.). The passages are well discussed by de Lugo, *de virt. fid. div.*, xix. 15 ; Suarez, *de fid. theol.*, xvii. 1, n. 4.

rejected a conclusion at once so harsh and so inequitable, compromising with the Augustinian only so far as to admit that, while the ignorance of the heathen world was not ' peccatum,' it might reasonably be regarded as ' poena peccati.' [1] Augustine in his kinder moments had treated ignorance as a fitting excuse for sin. ' You are not held responsible for involuntary ignorance,' he had written; [2] and had compared acts committed through ignorance to the stammering of an infant that has not yet learned to talk, which is not only inculpable in itself, but also ' humanis affectibus blanda et grata.' [3] So, too, Ambrose, in his funeral oration on the Emperor Valentinian, speaking of the indiscretions of youth which that great man had avoided, had said ' cito meretur veniam qui praetendit ignorantiam.' [4] Jerome, rigid moralist though he was, could write ' ignorantibus concedi veniam potest si, ad meliora conversi, scientiam in vobis doceatis fluctuasse, non studium.' [5] Passages in the Fathers which seemed to point in an opposite direction could not, of course, be ignored, but might easily be reinterpreted; Gratian, for example, deals readily enough with a passing remark of Ambrose which had caused difficulty. [6]

Common sense, however, is always a prey to the sophist, the sceptic, and the scrupulous. Proverbial wisdom is bound to be betrayed by its manifest exceptions. The doctrine of the blamelessness of ' sin ' committed in ignorance went unchallenged for long enough, applied as it was by rule-of-thumb methods in an environment not highly civilised or educated. But sooner or later someone was

---

[1] So, virtually, *S.T.*, i. 2, q. 87, a. 2 ; and explicitly Alexander of Hales, *S.T.*, ii, q. 113, m. 2 ; Suarez, *de fid. theol.*, xvii. 1, n. 14 ; de Lugo, *de virt. fid. div.*, xviii. 1, n. 25.

[2] *de lib. arb.*, iii. 19 (53).

[3] *Ib.* 22 (64).   Cf. *Retract.* i. 9 : ' All sin is voluntary.'

[4] *de ob. Val. consol.*, 13.

[5] *in ep. ad Gal.*, i. 3.

[6] See the ' dictum Gratiani ' in *Corp. Jur. Can.*, c. 12, C. I, q. 4.

sure to overstep the limits of sound common sense, and
claim ignorance as an excuse for inexcusable sin ; and
then the need for definition would be felt. The Church
would have to proclaim once and for all what kind of ignorance made deviation from the accepted path excusable,
and what kind did not. In this, as in so many other
respects, it was Abailard who drove the problem home.

## II

Abailard's ' Scito Teipsum ' fell like a bombshell upon a
Church which ambitious hierarchical schemes and a rapidly
spreading penitential system (fully equipped with cut-and-
dried manuals for confessors) had made predominantly
formalist. The main purpose of the book is to distinguish
both between natural evil tendencies (' vitia ') and a sinful
will (' peccatum ') ; and between the sinful consent of the
will and merely technical breaches of the law (' opera
peccati ').[1] Sin, the writer submits, is in the sinful consent
of the will alone, not in the evil tendencies as such, nor in
the externally lawless act (chap. ii). He therefore selects
instances of acts or desires lawless in themselves, but
blameless in common opinion because there is no real
consent of the will. The slave who has long gone in danger
of death at his master's hands, and at last in the extremity
of fear slays him, can only be regarded as morally guilty
by a perverse sophistry. In such a case not ' voluntas ' but
' passio ' causes the act. The man who covets his neighbour's fruit trees, but beats back the desire and refuses
to steal the fruit, is not held guilty either, though for the
time he has coveted. ' Quorsum autem ista ? ut denique

---

[1] This second distinction corresponds with that drawn later between
' formal ' and ' material ' sin ; ' material ' sin designating breaches of the
law not resulting from any sinful intention of the agent, ' formal ' sin,
breaches to which the agent's will is consciously a party.

pateat in talibus ipsam quoque voluntatem vel desiderium faciendi quod non licet nequaquam dici peccatum, sed ipsum potius, ut diximus, consensum ' (chap. iii.).

So far, though some of the examples he chooses press his doctrine to the extreme limits of reasonableness, he has kept within the bounds of orthodoxy ; and his third chapter in particular shows an exceptionally keen power of psychological analysis in its dissection of the stages of sin. After a digression on demonic temptation and the like (chap. iv.) he passes to the rationale of punishment ; and points out that the fact that actions, rather than intentions, are punished, is no proof that the latter are less culpable than the former. ' Non enim homines de occultis sed de manifestis judicant, nec tam culpae reatum quam operis pensant effectum.' ' Think of a poor woman with a babe unweaned,' he writes, ' who has not enough clothing to suffice both for herself and the little one in its cradle. . . . Moved by pity for the child, she catches it to herself to fold it in her own rags ; but nature overcomes her in her weakness, and she suffocates the babe whom she embraces in her extreme love. *Have love and do what you will*, Augustine said ; but when the woman comes before the bishop in confession (' pro satisfactione ') he imposes a severe penance upon her, not for any sin she has committed, but to warn her and other women to be more careful in such matters.' ' It is God alone,' he concludes, ' Who judges not so much what is done, as the purpose with which it is done ' (chap. v.).

The following chapters (vi., vii. and viii.) enlarge this theme. He then devotes three chapters to proving, by arguments which sometimes sound a trifle perverse, the parallel thesis that the consent of the will to what is good is good in itself, even though circumstances prevent its coming to good fruition. Then at length he approaches his central paradox. What of those who slew the martyrs, ' thinking to do God a service '—' having a zeal for God, but not according to knowledge ' ? [1] ' Some people' (with whom Abailard is about to identify himself) 'hold that so long as a man believes he is doing right and pleasing God, his intention is good and right.' But he foresees an objection. 'If a man is *deceived* by his zeal or enthusiasm,' it may be urged, ' his intention is erroneous ; the " eye of his heart " is not single ('simplex ') ; hence he cannot see clearly, or keep himself from error. So the Lord, in distinguishing actions by reference to the goodness or badness of the intention, spoke of the intention as being " single " (that is, unsullied, capable of seeing clearly) or " darkened." . . . Therefore '—the objector continues—'we must not call an intention good when it seems good < to the agent >, but only when it *is* as good as it seems ; when, that is to say, a man who thinks his purpose is pleasing to God is not deceived in his opinion. Otherwise infidels would have to be credited with good works as much as we Christians, for they no less than ourselves think they are being saved, or are pleasing God, by their works.'

Chapter xiii is headed ' quod peccatum non est nisi contra conscientiam.' First of all Abailard states his thesis : ' If you ask whether those persecutors of Christ and of the martyrs sinned in that which they thought would please God ; or whether they could without sin tolerate that which they thought intolerable, our definition of sin as " contempt of God " or " consent to something which we believe ought not to be consented to " makes it impossible for us to say that they sinned in this ; or that any man's ignorance, even though it be that infidelity itself which makes salvation impossible, is sinful. For those who know not Christ, and on that account reject the Christian faith, because they believe it contrary to God—how do they show contempt of God in what they do on God's behalf, thinking on that account that they are doing right ? '

[1] John xvi. 2 ; Rom. x. 2.

Then comes an objection drawn from Scripture: ' But
if their ignorance is in no way to be ascribed to sin, how
is it that the Lord Himself prays for those who crucify Him,
*Father, forgive them, for they know not what they do*; or that
Stephen, following His example, prays for those who stone
him with the words, *Lord, lay not this sin to their account*?
There is no need of forgiveness where there has been
no offence ; forgiveness means remitting ('condonare') a
penalty which guilt has earned. And Stephen definitely
uses the word " sin " of that which was done in ignorance.'

This objection, together with the former, Abailard
answers in chapter xiv. He begins by pointing out the
many different uses of the word ' sin '; and in this connection, after repeating that sin in the strict sense is ' contempt
of God or consent to evil,' reminds us that children and
' naturaliter stulti ' can never be guilty of it. It is not in
this sense, of genuine and deliberate offence against God,
that Stephen used the word of his accusers. He was
referring rather to ' poenam quam patiebatur ex peccato
primorum parentum,' or to ' injustam eorum actionem
quam habebant in lapidando.' So, too, the cry of ' Forgive
them ' from the cross need not refer to forgiveness in the
strict sense, as implying guilt. It can simply mean ' do
not requite it '—' ne vindices '; and its purpose was to
teach us patience and disinterested love. ' So therefore
what they did in ignorance cannot be called sin in the
strict sense : nor can their very ignorance itself. Nor can
infidelity (if it arise from ignorance) be sin, although it
necessarily excludes adults who have the use of reason from
eternal life. For,' he adds, and this is of extreme significance
both for later developments of the doctrine of invincible
ignorance [1] and for our estimate of Abailard's own orthodoxy,[2] ' not to believe the gospel, not to know Christ, not
to use the sacraments, must ensure damnation, even though

[1] *Infra*, chap. iii.          [2] *Infra*, p. 75.

the cause be not malice but ignorance.' Abailard's challenge
to tradition is obviously strictly limited ; but he does not
rest happily in his conclusion that inculpable ignorance
of the gospel will yet bring damnation.  He can only say :
' abyssus quippe multa Dei judicia sunt ; qui nonnumquam
reluctantes vel minus de salute sua sollicitos trahit, et se
offerentes vel ad credendum paratiores profundissimo
dispensationis suae consilio respuit.'

And so he comes to his conclusion.  ' " Sin " in the strict
sense can only be predicated of those who are guilty of
negligence ; and wherever *this* is found it is bound to bring
damnation.  But I cannot see that guilt is involved by
infidelity in the case of infants and those to whom the
gospel has never been preached, nor in any act which results
from invincible ignorance [1] and cannot therefore be foreseen ;
as for example if a huntsman kills some unseen person in a
wood with his arrow, thinking he is shooting at beasts and
birds.  We may say that he " sins " through ignorance, but
that is only a loose use of the word. . . . Such " sin " through
ignorance cannot involve guilt. . . . So if those who perse-
cuted Christ and His followers did so because they thought
the latter were worthy of persecution, we may say that
they " sinned " in this loose sense ; but they would have
sinned more gravely and with real guilt (' gravius culpam

[1] This is the earliest appearance of the actual phrase ' invincible
ignorance ' which I have met with.  In previous discussions of the subject
in which it might have been expected to occur it is absent.  Thus in the
letter of Nicolas I to Hinckmar of Rheims, A.D. 863 (quoted by Gratian,
*Corp. Jur. Can.*, c. 102, C. XI, q. 3), ' simulated ' and ' voluntary ' ignorance are mentioned, and a type of ignorance identical with what was later
called ' invincible ' is expressly distinguished from them.  The word
' invincibilis ' is not classical, and the lexicons give only two post-classical
examples, from Tertullian and Apuleius respectively.  It reappears in the
twelfth century in other connections besides the present one—thus Robert
Pullen (*Sent.*, v, cc. 32, 33, 34) uses it to express the ineradicable quality
attaching to the first motions towards sin ; Thomas of Ely (Mabillon,
*Acta SS. ord. S. Ben.*, ii. 749) of Queen Etheldreda's ' invincible ' deter-
mination to take the veil.  Thereafter it is in common use.

peccassent ') if they had spared them against the dictates of their conscience.'

We need not follow the course of the book further, for after two transitional chapters on venial sin, it diverges into a discussion of the sacrament of penance which has nothing to our purpose.   The material already quoted is sufficiently startling, and constituted a challenge which had to be taken up.   The suggestion that those who crucified Christ were guiltless revolted the moral sense of Christianity ; the suggestion that ignorance could be an excuse for any sin whatever seemed to open up a very abyss of potential wickedness and antinomianism.   So far from attempting to conciliate the opposition he was bound to meet with, Abailard had done his best to provoke it.   To prove his thesis that motive and not consequence is the important factor in morality, he had gone out of his way to assert that ' sometimes it is right for us to do what God forbids, just as sometimes God lays down precepts which it would be wrong to obey.'   He takes, for example, the case of those whom the Lord forbade to speak of the miracles He had done, ' but the more He forbade them the more they published it abroad.' It was right for Him to forbid ' as an example of humility, lest anyone should seek glory on account of such grace given to him ;  but they were not wrong in disobeying, since they did it in His honour '—' fuit bonum praecipi quod non fuit bonum fieri.'   So, too, Jehovah's command to Abraham to kill Isaac was a just command, ' to prove his obedience and constancy of faith and love ' ;  but the action commanded was in itself ' not good.' [1]   He resumes the paradox with other examples in the ' Dialogue ' [2] : ' It often happens that a good thing is done, but not done well. . . . Two men may hang a criminal, the one solely out of hate for him ;  the other in the execution of justice.   The hanging is just ;  but the one man does it justly, because with the right intention ;

<hr>

[1] Chap. iii.                              [2] Ed. V. Cousin, ii. 711.

the other unjustly, because through no love for justice, but through sheer anger and hate.' Abailard had fixed unerringly upon the weak spot in all legalism, but his treatment of the subject proved a severe trial for the simpler minds of his day.

It was easy enough to condemn the doctrine ; and this was done at the instigation of William of St. Thierry [1] and St. Bernard [2] at the Council of Sens.[3] But to meet the argument with counter-argument was a very different matter. Two questions specially arose for discussion : (1) What are the limits, if any, within which ignorance may properly be regarded as invincible and inculpable ? and (2) Are there any principles of conduct which can be wholly withdrawn from the shelter of this excuse—of which *no man* can be invincibly ignorant ? To the solution of these questions scholasticism addressed itself. Two stages in the development of a full theory are marked respectively by the contributions of Alexander of Hales and St. Thomas Aquinas.

## III

Alexander of Hales († 1245) approaches the question of ignorance from the point of view of ' delicta,' or sins of omission (' derelictio boni faciendi '—a curious piece of nomenclature, derived from the ' Glossa Ordinaria ' on Psalm xxxii. 5,[4] of which later writers did not make much use).[5] He divides ' delicta ' into three kinds—ignorance, omission, and negligence.[6] ' Ignorance ' is a word which has many meanings—but at the outset we can say that where it involves voluntary refusal to know what is necessary to

---

[1] *Epp. S. Bern.*, no. 326.

[2] *Epp.* 188, 190 (see especially the *capitula haeresum*, 10, 11, 13).

[3] Denzinger-Bannwart, *Enchiridion*[14], no. 377.

[4] Alex. Halens., *Summa*, ii, q. 112, *init.*

[5] There is a passing reference to it in Aquinas, *S.T.*, ii. 2, q. 79, a. 4, obj. 1.

[6] q. 113, *init.*

salvation it is of course a sin.[1] Its relation to ' error ' is that
the latter consists in definite assent to something untrue,
or dissent from something true ; whereas the former is
mere absence of knowledge without in itself involving assent
or dissent.[2] One or two other distinctions of minor importance follow. In the 6th ' member ' of question 113 he
comes to grips with his subject : ' Is ignorance (as Ambrose
infers from Romans ii. 4, *Not knowing the goodness of God*) the
worst of all sins ? ' To this he replies : ' Ignorance may be
spoken of as a sin in different ways. A man may sin without
knowing it ; then he sins from ignorance. He may sin without knowing it, or caring to know it, or without a recognition
of the gravity of his sin ; thus he becomes insensible both
to the guilt and to its condemnation. So ignorance may
dispose a man to commit a sin ; or be the actual material of
the sin ; or follow the sin and aggravate it.' This is obscure,
but St. Thomas will clear it up for us by his distinctions
between ' antecedent,' ' concomitant ' and ' consequent '
ignorance. We can pass on to the central problem : ' Does
ignorance excuse from sin ? ' (membr. 7), and, if so, ' Do
some kinds of ignorance excuse more than others ? '
(membr. 8).

Alexander at once attacks the problem of invincible
ignorance, but is led into a further digression on various
kinds of ignorance. ' Ignorance is <sometimes> invincible
in the circumstances (' ex casu '), (into which a man falls
through no fault of his own), or [3] from the weakness of nature ;
and this excuses. Again, there is ignorance of divine
law and of canon law, and this excuses the uninstructed
(' simplices ') as far as those principles are concerned
knowledge of which is not necessary for salvation. On the
other hand there is an ignorance which does not excuse in so
far as God is concerned (' quoad Deum '), as for example
" supine " ignorance, or " affected " (' affectata '), and igno-

---

[1] Alex. Halens., *ut supra*, q. 113, m. 1.    [2] *Ib.*, m. 3.
[3] Reading *vel*. The variant *sed* gives an inferior sense.

rance of those things which a man is required ('tenetur')
to know, and the ignorance of negligence.'

'Membrum' 8 attempts to introduce order into these
confused observations. And first as to 'ignorance of law.'
'Even though it excuses anyone (as it certainly does in the
case of those who have no opportunity of being skilled in it ;
children for example, and rustics and women), it excuses less
than ignorance of fact.' Alexander does not dwell on this
point ; its truth is obvious to him. 'Ignorance of law,' he
goes on, 'provides less excuse in matters affecting salvation :
for example ignorance of canon and divine law (at all events
as far as certain precepts are concerned). Ignorance of the
natural law provides the least excuse of all ; ignorance of
canon law is more excusable in some persons, and ignorance of
civil law <even> more so. For the more a man is required
to know a law, the less does ignorance of it provide an excuse.
Now everyone is required to have a knowledge of the
natural law—therefore no adult can plead ignorance of it as
an excuse ; for no adult may be ignorant ('licet ignorare')
of the natural law, since it is naturally written upon the
hearts of everyone.'

It is interesting to notice how the concept of the 'natural
law' is called in as a bulwark. There are some moral principles of which no man can be ignorant. They are innate in
all of us ; here is a fact against which no plea of invincible
ignorance can avail. The idea of 'natural law' has time
and again proved an invaluable ally both to conservatives
and to revolutionaries. Abailard had used it in the revo-
lutionary interest to extend the faith beyond its apparent
limits of the Church ; [1] the thirteenth century appeals to it

[1] Thus in the *Dialogue* it is the pagan philosopher who is made to say:
'summum bonum apud omnes recte philosophantes non aliud quam Deum
dici constat et credi . . . summum autem hominis bonum illa est perpetua
quies sive laetitia quam quisque pro meritis post hanc vitam recipit, sive
in ipsa visione vel cognitione Dei, ut dicitis, sive quoquo modo aliter
contingat' (Cousin, ii. 691). The Christian interlocutor merely fills out
the scheme. See *infra*, p. 75.

in defence of orthodoxy. Alexander does not develop the thought, but goes on to consider other cases in which ignorance of law cannot be regarded as an excuse. Bishops and ' major prelates ' are required (' tenentur ') to know the ' divine law,'—that is the Old and New Testaments,—because they must be able to give everyone who asks a reason for the faith and hope which is in them. Laymen are bound in the same way to know the decalogue and the creeds. Parish priests and confessors must know their canon law; other clerics may safely be ignorant of parts of it. Ignorance of law, then, may or may not be an excuse; all depends upon how far the offender was required by his position or engagements to obtain a knowledge of the law.

A similar distinction meets us when we turn to ' ignorance of facts.' There are some facts of which we are required to be certain; the Christian for his soul's salvation must know that Christ died for him, the priest must be sure that he is validly ordained before he presumes to minister. Other facts are indifferent; since St. Paul's time it has not mattered to the Christian to know whether the meat he eats was offered to an idol or not. Where we are dealing with laws or facts of which we are bound to be certain, ignorance therefore can never provide a full excuse, except in the case (which Alexander notices in passing) of a total incapacity for knowledge, like that of lifelong insanity. Even so, some kinds of ignorance are more heinous than others. ' Simple ' ignorance—' when a man does something, but not all that he might '—is not a full excuse, but it is better than ' crass ' ignorance, which arises from definite though not deliberate negligence. And ' crass ' ignorance is not so bad as ' affected '; for ' affected ' ignorance is not an excuse but an aggravation of the offence, because it denotes ignorance which comes from deliberate and intentional negligence.

Despite the prolixity and apparent confusion of this discussion, Alexander has really established two points.

The first is, that ignorance of the natural law can never be an excuse for actions in contravention of it ; for that law is written on men's hearts.  The second is, that ignorance of what a person is *bound* to know is an equally futile plea ; though here there are degrees of culpability according to the degree of complacency with which the culprit regards his ignorance, and of the negligence from which it arises.  The threatened moral chaos has thus been averted ; Abailard's scepticism is fairly hedged in.  It might be urged for example (though Alexander does not urge it) that the authorities who crucified Christ were bound by their position to conduct the trial fairly, and to make such enquiries as (in this case) would have established His innocence beyond all chance of cavil.[1]

But moral laxity might still remain unchecked unless the plea of ignorance, in matters which one cannot in general regard oneself as strictly bound to know, is equally hedged in.  Here Alexander is less satisfying.  He knows of ' invincible ' and of ' involuntary ' ignorance, but he is not clear as to the relation between them, and his discussion is slight and confined to technicalities.  Of invincible ignorance he repeats that it sometimes arises by nature, ' as in a boy who has not reached the use of reason ; in an old man, who cannot < any longer > draw distinctions ; or in a man born insane.'  In all these cases it provides a complete excuse.  On the other hand it may arise from the circumstances of a particular case (' ex casu ') ; and here we must distinguish between ignorance for which the agent is responsible, and that for which he is not responsible (' quae incidit ex sua culpa—non ex sua culpa ').  ' Of these the latter excuses completely ; the former according to some authorities does not excuse from entire blame, according to others it does.'

[1] St. Thomas actually suggests this line of reply to Abailard, by referring to the problem of those who slew the apostles 'thinking to do God a service ' in connection with the discussion of ignorance arising out of negligence (i 2, q. 19, a. 6 : *infra*, p. 27).

We hesitate rightly to accept the theorem that any ignorance can be called 'invincible' which arises out of the agent's own fault : for though we have not yet reached a definition of invincibility the statement would appear to be a contradiction in terms.  But once again St. Thomas will come to the rescue ; and as a matter of fact Alexander indicates his meaning in the succinct sentence : ' jam non habet usum rationis, sed prius non excusabatur, sive de priori.'  He is thinking of cases in which a man is responsible for getting into a condition in which ignorance is an inevitable (i.e. invincible) sequel.  The drunkard may commit a whole catalogue of crimes in the passion of intoxication without knowing it ; but he was responsible for allowing himself to become drunk.  The moral problem is here very complicated.  How far does the offender's responsibility go ?  Is he to be blamed for drunkenness only, or for any or all of the offences committed under the influence of drink ?  And if for the latter, is he to be blamed as much as if he had been sober ?  No wonder that the authorities to whom Alexander refers disagree on the point.

He passes on to the subject of involuntary ignorance, dealing with ' voluntary ' ignorance by the way.  He has forgotten his former distinction between ' simple,' ' crass,' and ' affected ' ignorance ; and now divides voluntary ignorance into ' affectata simpliciter ' and ' affectata secundum quid.'  The former is the ignorance of those who ' will not to know,' the latter of those who ' do not will to know.'  The former therefore is the more heinous of the two ; the latter is identical with what was previously called ' crass ' ignorance.  Of involuntary ignorance he has no more to say than that it is sometimes involuntary from the outset ; this is not ' peccatum ' but ' poena ' (i.e. the outcome of original sin) and ' excusat a toto.'  At other times it was voluntary to start with, but became involuntary, and this excuses from a part but not altogether.

Here his mind has gone back to the case of the drunkard ; and in stating as his own position that such ignorance ' excuses in part ' he has adopted a middle position among the authorities of whom he has spoken.

This discussion of ' invincible ' and ' involuntary ' ignorance shows a marked falling off from the clearness which characterised the previous consideration of ignorance of law and of fact. Alexander belongs to a phase of thought in which, while it was quite clear that some kinds of ignorance do *not* excuse for sins committed under their influence, it was not at all clear what kinds of ignorance *might* excuse. If you are ignorant of natural law, or of any law or fact of which your position or circumstances morally require you to be cognisant, you are not merely guilty of the sin of ignorance itself, but fully responsible also for any and every consequence that may follow. If, on the other hand, your ignorance of a relevant law or fact was wholly unavoidable and unintentional, you are in no way responsible for any of the consequences. But between these two extremes lies a vast field of undetermined cases. Where you might have known a relevant principle or fact, but were not morally bound by your circumstances to know it, what degree of responsibility is yours if ignorance of it leads you into ' sin ' ? Where, again, sin or negligence brings you into a condition in which you completely lose sight of a known principle or fact, or fail to recognise a new fact which should bear upon your action, it is clear that you are responsible for falling into that condition ; but do you incur also responsibility for all the consequences which may arise ? In problems such as these Alexander is wholly at a loss, and his attempts to deal with ' invincible ' and ' involuntary ' ignorance only increase the confusion in his mind. Scholasticism had not as yet fought its way to a principle applicable to such cases. That Alexander himself was conscious of his failure in such matters is shown by the fact that he appends to his discussion ' ad majorem evidentiam '—' to make it clearer '—certain cases of ignorance.

With these we need not concern ourselves deeply. There is the case of the boy brought up in ignorance of the faith ' in carcere Saracenorum '—a boy whom we shall meet again as the ' puer perveniens ' of St. Thomas. There is the problem as to how far a man ought to know all about mortal sin, particularly in ' subtle cases of simony ' ; and that of the priest who with the best will in the world cannot remember his canon law. On neither of these questions is Alexander very explicit. But one of his cases is important, not because it is of common occurrence, but because the solution shows a vestige of principle behind it, which later writers seized upon and developed. ' Again we are asked,' he says, ' about the man to whom Satan appears disguised as an angel of light.[1] The man believes him to be an angel of light ; he exercises all the diligence he can <to discover if he is so or no> and <finally> worships him. Is he excused by ignorance ? ' ' It would seem that he is,' is the first reply, ' because he has exercised all the diligence he could.' ' But,' continues the objector, ' he is adoring someone whom he ought not to adore : therefore he sins.' Here is the case. Alexander solves it in the best scholastic manner : ' I reply that he has not exercised all the diligence he might ; if he had, either he would have recognised the truth himself, or God would have revealed it to him.' The importance of this test of ' diligence ' will appear later.

## IV

Alexander, we must conclude, is more competent at stating difficulties and giving a rough-and-ready solution, than at discovering the principles involved. He has left

[1] A favourite question ; see Aug., *Enchir.*, 60 ; Aquinas, *S.T.*, ii. 2, q. 10, a. 2.

us little of value except his clear conviction that ignorance of the natural law, and of things one is morally bound to know, can never be excusable in itself or in its consequences. St. Thomas, though far less interested in particular cases, is much more informing on questions of principle.[1] He approaches the question of ignorance with greater circumspection, and from three successive points of view. He takes it first of all in connection with the question, ' What is the subject-matter of moral judgments ? ' again, in relation to the problem, ' What is the moral criterion ? ' and for the third time in relation to that of the excuses, if any, which can be accepted for a lapse from virtue. The three problems overlap, as is evident ; yet each is a question by itself, and each throws new light upon the difficulties connected with ignorance. The influence of the ' Nicomachean Ethics ' is obvious. In question six of the ' Prima Secundae ' he aims, as Aristotle did,[2] at limiting moral judgments to voluntary action. Like Aristotle, he begins by ruling out actions caused by violence ; and faces the problem of acts committed solely under the influence of fear (aa. 5, 6). Article 7 deals with the degree of responsibility incurred by acts committed in moments of passion.[3] These discussed, he is free to consider the problem of ignorance ; and in article 8 puts the question, ' utrum ignorantia causet involuntarium ? '

The ' objections ' to the affirmative answer are mainly scriptural,[4] though, as we have seen, great play might

---

[1] Albert the Great had also dealt with the subject, curiously enough in the special connection of the sin of Adam. His discussion throws little new light upon it, though he slightly develops the conception of invincible ignorance *ex natura* by adding ' sicut in morionibus et melancholicis ' (*Summa*, ii, q. 88).

[2] *Eth. Nic.*, iii. 1.

[3] Cf. *Eth. Nic.*, iii. 1. 14.

[4] 1 Cor. xiv. 38: ' si quis ignorat, ignorabitur ' ; Prov. xiv. 22: ' errant, qui operantur malum ' (hence all sin is the result of ignorance, and if ignorance makes an act involuntary, all sin would be inculpable).

have been made with the authority of Augustine. One objection however introduces an important point : ignorance can only be thought to excuse if enlightenment brings regret and repentance (' tristitia ').[1] The man who slays an enemy thinking he is slaying a stag cannot plead ignorance if he wanted to kill his enemy anyhow, and is without regret when he knows the result. This enables St. Thomas to lay down his first ' division ' of ignorance, into *antecedent, concomitant,* and *consequent,* which clears up one of Alexander's confusions. These technicalities will puzzle us only if we fail to realise that they refer to the relation of the ignorance not to the act committed, but to the will of the agent.[2] Ignorance is called ' concomitant ' where, ' though it accompanies the act, the act would still be done even if the facts were known. [3] Such ignorance does not influence the will to commit the act ; it merely happens that act and ignorance go together. . . . And so, as Aristotle says,[4] such ignorance does not make an act involuntary because it causes nothing which is genuinely repugnant to the will ; but only " non-voluntary "'—a term which (as Aristotle pointed out, though St. Thomas ignores the remark) is of value merely as indicating a separate species of action, but does not in any way imply inculpability.

' Consequent ' ignorance is ' ignorance which itself is voluntary,' as for example when the will to an act paves the way by a voluntary ignoring of the principles or facts which, if recognised, would make the act sinful ; or when (without any consciously willed ignoring of what is relevant)

---

[1] This is Aristotle's ἐπίλυπον καὶ ἐν μεταμελείᾳ (*Eth.*, iii. 1). Cp. Albertus Magnus, *Eth.*, iii, tr. 1, c. 8 : ' hoc est involuntarium, quando factum triste est et *poenitudine* voluntati secundum se contrarium.'

[2] ' Ad actum voluntatis ' rather than ' ad motum voluntatis ad aliquid agendum.'

[3] ' Quando ignorantia est de eo quod agitur, tamen etiam si sciretur, nihilominus ageretur.'

[4] *Eth.*, iii. 1. 13.

a man fails to consider in action what he might and should consider, or suffers from an ignorance induced by habit or passion. In all these cases (of which ' ignorance of the universal principles of law ' [1] is one of the most notable examples) the ignorance is voluntary, though it may arise either from deliberate exclusion of relevant fact in a particular case, or from general negligence. It is true that such ignorance is ' antecedent ' to the act, but it is ' consequent ' to an act of will bearing upon itself with a view to facilitating that particular act or acts of that character in general ; hence the technical term. And so, if it can be said at all to make an act involuntary, it does so only ' secundum quid.'

Lastly we come to ' antecedent ' ignorance. Here the ignorance is genuinely involuntary, and precedes any act of the will directed either towards securing or maintaining a condition of ignorance, or to committing a particular action. ' For example, when a man does not know some circumstance of an act which he was not bound to know, and so acts in a way in which he would not have acted had he known ; as for example if after careful investigation (' diligentia adhibita ') he still does not know that some-one is coming along the road, and so shoots an arrow which kills him ; ignorance of this kind makes the action completely involuntary.'

St. Thomas has thus, like his predecessor, delimited the scope of the enquiry, without involving himself in that predecessor's confusion. The plea of ignorance can never be admitted as a total excuse for a ' sinful ' act where (1) knowledge would not have prevented the action, and (2) the ignorance was in any degree itself the result of intention or negligence, either in general or directed to this particular case. Incidentally he has established or

[1] This is really from *Eth.*, iii. 1. 15 : οὐ γὰρ ἡ ἐν τῇ προαιρέσει ἄγνοια αἰτία τοῦ ἀκουσίου ἀλλὰ τῆς μοχθηρίας, οὐδ' ἡ καθόλου, ψέγονται γὰρ διά γε ταύτην.

confirmed two further principles—ignorance of the universal truths of the (natural) law is never an excuse; and
regret for the action done is a useful rough-and-ready
test to apply in all cases—for where there is no regret
there can be no excuse. Aristotle, in the passage on
which the Schoolmen depended, had dwelt on both these
points.

The second discussion of ignorance (i. 2, q. 19) overlaps
the first to some extent, but also produces new features of importance. In question 20 St. Thomas is going to discuss the
all-important problem (raised as we have seen by Abailard)
how far the morality of an act is determined *solely* by the
state of will of the agent; and how far (if at all) the actual
consequences supply any additional criterion? As a preliminary he asks, How can we decide whether the will of
the agent is good? In articles 1 and 2 he points out that
what makes the will good or bad is its ' object ' (' motive '
or ' purpose '); in article 3 he adds that this ' object ' is
presented to the will by reason. A good will is one which
aims at that which reason presents as good, or which is in
accordance with reason. But (a. 4) is this merely a doctrinaire assertion, or has it its roots in some deep underlying
principle? St. Thomas finds its justification in the statement (itself perhaps doctrinaire, but inherent in his
entire system of philosophy) that ' the human reason is
derived from the divine,' and consequently is the mirror
of eternal truth. And here the new form of the problem
begins. It is pitiably evident that human reason and
eternal truth do not always correspond, as ideally they
should. So long as he trusts his reason an individual will
never be conscious that it is out of line with the will of God;
but others, watching him, advising him, may see it to be so.
How are they to judge of his ' will ' in such a case? Are
they to say, To obey your reason when it is wrong
(even though you cannot be conscious that it is wrong)

is sinful ; or on the other hand, To disobey your reason,
*even* when it is wrong, is sinful ?   So article 5 puts
the question, ' Whether a will which disobeys (' discordans
ab ') reason when it is wrong is bad ? ' and article 6 :
' Whether a will obeying reason when it is wrong is
good ? '

St. Thomas tells us that these two questions are identical
with the questions :  ' Does a conscience in error oblige (to
action) ? ' and ' Does a conscience in error excuse ? '—
though it might fairly be suggested that ' justify ' would be
a better word than ' excuse ' in the second statement.   This
turn of the argument, by which attention is concentrated
upon ' conscience ' rather than upon ' ignorance,' is of
supreme importance for later developments.   Conscience
to him, both in its preceptive and in its judicial character,
is a fully intellectual activity.   In its former character it
' investigates by means of knowledge what should be done,
as though we were taking counsel ;  and so resembles the
process of discovery (' inventio ') by which we argue from
principles to conclusions.   In the latter character, it
resembles the process by which we refer conclusions to their
principles.' [1]   In answer to the first question he dismisses
the argument that where conscience erroneously prescribes
something by nature indifferent (as ' picking up a straw from
the ground ') it must be obeyed, but where the action
prescribed is wrong it does not ' oblige,' by pointing out that
if conscience is in error even an indifferent action is in some
sense bad—there is no difference between the two cases
Can we say then that an erroneous conscience must be
disobeyed ?   Anything but that ;  for conscience is the only
guide that a man has ;  to disobey is to act contrary to
reason, and this in itself is evil.   ' And so the Philosopher
says, that strictly speaking the incontinent man is one who
disobeys right reason, but by accident he may be one who

---

[1] *de ver.*, xvii. 1.   Cp. *S.T.*, i, q. 79, a. 13.

disobeys reason even when wrong.'[1]   ' Hence,' St. Thomas concludes, ' we must say without qualification that every <act of> will in disobedience to reason, whether the latter be right or wrong, is always bad.'[2]

This conclusion is inevitable if we realise (what St. Thomas has not here asserted) that there is no question of a conscious conflict between conscience and law. An erroneous conscience is not one which knowingly holds an opinion contrary to law, but one which holds its opinion without the knowledge that the law has ever expressed itself on the point. ' Error ' to St. Thomas (as to Alexander) is simply an enhanced form of ignorance. ' Error adds something to ignorance. Ignorance may exist without a definite judgment about the thing ignored—it is then ignorance and not error : but when we pass a false judgment *about things which we do not know*, then our condition is properly called one of error.'[3]   You may not know that stealing is wrong—that is mere ignorance ; but if *in addition to not knowing that it is wrong* you believe that it is right, you have added error to ignorance. The case of holding something to be right which you know the Church holds to be wrong is simply not discussed at this point.

The answer to the second question ('Whether an erroneous conscience excuses ? ')[4] depends on the earlier discussion in question 6. If the error arose out of genuinely involuntary ignorance, ' absque omni negligentia,' the excuse is complete ; where it arose from some degree of negligence, there

---

[1] *Eth.*, vii. 2. 7, 9. The argument is however really brought forward by Aristotle's opponents, who urge that ' incontinence ' may sometimes be a good thing.   Aristotle's answer (vii. 3. 10) is designed to show that in some cases there may be an element of ' reason ' on both sides.   To have noticed this would have led St. Thomas into a discussion of the ' perplexed ' conscience, which he here avoids.

[2] This is more fully discussed, *de ver.*, xvii. 4. The conclusion is the same, with the refined distinction that the erroneous conscience binds only *per accidens*—i.e. so long as conscience remains confirmed in its error.

[3] *de mal.*, iii. 7.

[4] q. 19, a. 6.

is responsibility, but its degree will depend on further consideration. In the meantime a new point has been established. St. Thomas does not propose to consider the problem of ignorance apart from that of conscientiousness. Mere conscientiousness alone is not in itself an excuse for every kind of sinful action. Conscience must indeed be obeyed ; but its failure in any given case to warn its possessor as to the sinfulness of the act which he contemplates may itself arise from culpable causes. Conscience, in scriptural language, may be ' seared,' ' darkened,' or ' defiled ' [1] by voluntary negligence, or by infirmity or passion. But setting this aside, St. Thomas's clear principle is that anything less than conscientiousness is wrong ; if you are engaged in an action which you know or suspect to be immoral, the action cannot in any circumstances be inculpable. It is clear from q. 76, a. 4, that St. Thomas would not have taken up the rigorist position that in *all* circumstances a man is responsible for *all* the consequences of a sinful act—a position resulting in the maxim ' qui ex culpa levi causavit grave damnum, tenetur sub mortali ad reparationem totius damni.' [2] But he is not prepared at this point to discuss the degree of responsibility for actions in which guilt of some kind is patently and admittedly present ; he leaves this to the refined subtleties of the casuists.[3] He is in search of the

---

[1] 1 Tim. iv. 2 ; Eph. iv. 18 ; Tit. i. 15. In *de ver.*, xvii. 1, ad 2, 3, St. Thomas discusses the ' defiled ' conscience, but curiously enough treats it as meaning only a ' guilty ' conscience.

[2] Quoted, Prümmer, *Manuale Theol. Mor.*, ii, p. 88, where the maxim is described as ' now obsolete.'

[3] The question is usually discussed under the heading *de restitutione ex injusta damnificatione*. Gury-Ferreres, *Compendium Theol. Mor.*, i, pp. 483–484, puts together the principal test problems and the authorities on either side. Cases discussed are : the degree of responsibility of one who, in error, has slandered another ; of the priest who (in contravention of ecclesiastical law) has gone shooting, and accidentally injured someone ; of one who, intending to injure A, has injured B by mistake ; or intending to injure A slightly has injured him seriously ; or by his bad example or advice has unintentionally caused someone else to do wrong ; or finds that another is suspected for his own crimes etc.

principles which establish complete inculpability as the result of ignorance ; and there can be no complete inculpability where conscience has been violated.

By ' conscience ' (and therefore by ' conscientiousness ') St. Thomas means something rigorous : a judgment as final, in its own sphere, as the judgments of science or logic with which he has definitely compared it. The later distinction between the ' certain ' and the ' doubtful ' conscience is wholly unknown to him. An ' opinion ' or ' idea ' framed under the influence of ignorance cannot shelter under the cloak of that ignorance if the consequences are evil. An erroneous conscience *may* in certain cases excuse ; that an erroneous opinion or fancy should in *any* case excuse is not even considered a thesis worth discussion.

## V

So far we have established negative conclusions only. There can be no genuine inculpability where the act committed is in contravention of a ' law of nature ' ; nor yet where conscience has been violated ; nor where enlightenment does not bring regret. But suppose that in all these respects the required conditions are satisfied, in what cases, if any, does ignorance or error completely excuse from guilt ? To this St. Thomas addresses himself (taking up by the way one or two hints he has already dropped) in a third discussion, arising primarily out of the consideration of the causes of sin [1]—sin being in the widest sense *any* ' word, act, or thought ' (intentional or otherwise) ' contrary to the divine law.' [2]  On a psychological basis he divides the ' internal ' causes of sin into three—ignorance (failure of the reason) ; infirmity (disorder of the ' sensitive appetite ') ;

[1] i. 2, qq. 75, 76.   W. H. V. Reade, *Moral System of Dante's Inferno*, pp. 239 ff., is a valuable commentary on this discussion.
[2] q. 71, a. 6.

and ' malice ' (disorder of the will). He has little difficulty
in showing (q. 76, a. 1) that ignorance can be a cause of the
' act of sin,' because it is ' the lack of such knowledge as
perfects reason, which prohibits the act of sin in so far as it
guides human action.' Ignorance, however, may be twofold
—either of general principles or of particular facts : you may
be (' materially ') guilty of parricide either because you are
unaware that it is forbidden, or because you do not know
that ' this man is your father.' This enables St. Thomas to
recall in a different form what he has said of ' concomitant '
ignorance ; your ignorance that the man you slay is your
father will not be the *cause* (and consequently not the
excuse) of your killing your father, unless the knowledge
that he was your father (had you known it) would have
restrained you—' talis non peccat propter ignorantiam, sed
peccat ignorans.'

Article 2 considers the question, ' Whether ignorance
itself is a sin ? ' Here he distinguishes ignorance from
' nescience,' following upon Isidore of Seville [1] (whom however he does not quote). Nescience is any kind of absence
of knowledge ; ignorance, absence of such kind of knowledge
as a man has the capacity of acquiring (' quae aptus natus
est scire '). This distinction is followed by another, which
we noticed previously in Alexander of Hales : there are,
among the things which a man is able to acquire, some which
he is bound (morally) to acquire—those namely which are
necessary for the discharge of his proper functions (' debitum
actum exercere '). ' Thus all men are bound to know the
things which are of faith, and the universal precepts of
law ; individuals are bound to know whatever appertains
(' ea quae spectant ') to their respective state or office.' As
distinct from ignorance of such matters is ignorance of
things which, though I am capable of knowing them, I am
not bound to know.

---

[1] *Differentiae*, sub lit. ' I.'

These two distinctions enable him to narrow his field yet further.   Ignorance of things which a man is bound to know is always culpable ; there is no further question about that. On the other hand, ignorance (or better, nescience) of things which one can never know—'ignorance which it is not in our power to repel '—cannot be imputed to negligence. Here at length St. Thomas introduces the word we have been expecting : ' Ignorance of this kind is called *invincible* ignorance, because it cannot be overcome by diligence ' (' studio superari non potest ') and therefore ' invincible ignorance can never be sin.' [1]   Vincible ignorance, on the other hand, if of things which we are morally bound to know, is sinful.   That leaves us with one question only : What of ignorance of those things which we *might have* known, but which, though relevant in the particular case, we were not *bound* to know by any general consideration arising out of our ' state or office ' ?   To our surprise, St. Thomas closes the material part of the discussion in this article (a. 2) with the curt remark that ' such ignorance is not sin.'   But he is thinking only of ignorance of things that are wholly irrelevant in any particular case ; there is more to be said where their relevance is obvious or even probable.

So article 3 restates the problem in the form, ' Does ignorance excuse entirely from sin ? '   After recalling principles we have already grasped, he continues as follows :

[1] This clears up one of the confusions noticed earlier in Alexander of Hales (*supra*, p. 18).   He had spoken of an invincible ignorance which does *not* excuse ; because the man has (vincibly) allowed himself to get into such a state that his ignorance, formerly vincible, is now invincible.   St. Thomas evades the difficulty by confining the idea of ' invincibility ' to ' ignorance which it is not in our power to repel ' ;   Alexander's doubtful cases (the drunkard etc.) he virtually considers under the head of ' conscience,' dismissing them by saying that ' clearness of conscience ' is not in itself an excuse unless this ' clearness ' results from no guilt or negligence— i.e. is not mere callousness or animality.   This makes it possible for him to see that not one but *three* factors are involved if the act is to be inculpable : (1) a clear conscience resulting from (2) no negligence in the education of conscience and (3) invincible ignorance.   He has some further interesting remarks on the drunkard in q. 76, a. 4.

'Sometimes ignorance does not wholly excuse from sin, and that from one of two causes. (1) The cause may lie in the thing which is ignored. . . . Thus a person may ignore some circumstance of a <sinful> act, knowledge of which would have prevented his committing the act, whether that circumstance is germane to the essence of the sin ('faciat ad rationem peccati') or not; yet there may remain in his consciousness something which leads him to recognise sinfulness in the act. Thus you may strike someone knowing him to be a man (and that in itself makes the act essentially sinful—'sufficit ad rationem peccati'), without knowing that he is your father—a circumstance which constitutes a new species of sin <and which, if you had known it, would have deterred you from striking him at all, and so from committing either sin>. Or, again, you may not know that the man is going to strike back; if you knew it, you would not strike him; but this fact does not affect the essential sinfulness of the act ('non pertinet ad rationem peccati'). <In either case> you sin through ignorance, but you are not wholly excused from sin, because to some extent ('adhuc') you still retained a consciousness of the sin.' Here St. Thomas has repeated his principle that where conscience has been violated no degree of ignorance can remove culpability; but he has hinted at a possible limitation of culpability to the sin intended, as distinct from all its consequences, a theme which he is to pursue further in article 4.

' (2) The cause may lie in the character of the ignorance itself. The ignorance may be voluntary—either directly, as when you deliberately neglect to inform yourself of something in order that you may sin more freely' (in article 4 he will insist that such ignorance—which we have already seen to be called 'affected'—*increases* the guilt of the consequent sin); 'or indirectly, as when through pressure of work and other occupations, you neglect to learn something which might have restrained you from the sin. Such negligence <direct or indirect>, in so far as it concerns things which one is bound and able to know, makes the ignorance, and so the sin, voluntary. It does not therefore wholly excuse from sin. But ignorance which is wholly involuntary, either because invincible or because we were not bound to acquire the knowledge in question, excuses entirely from sin.'

This is disappointing. Our problem was to discover some principle which would guide in cases where 'sin' arises from ignorance of something relevant and material, which nevertheless one is not by one's 'state or office' bound to know ; and St. Thomas gives us no guidance. He passes on, in article 4, to discuss the degree of culpability attaching to what Alexander had called 'supine,' 'crass,' and 'affected' ignorance respectively. We can only infer from this apparent omission that to him any knowledge relevant to (at all events) the immediate consequences of the act you contemplate, is knowledge which by your 'state or office' you are bound to acquire if possible. This type of case falls therefore under the general principles already considered ; 'state or office' must be taken in a wide sense as covering 'circumstances' in general. That St. Thomas did as a fact recognise this type of case is shown by a curious turn which he has given to his definition of invincible ignorance. Knowledge such as is demanded by one's 'condition or office' is *primarily* a knowledge of principles ; knowledge relevant to a particular case is *primarily* a knowledge of its 'circumstances,'[1] or of definite facts. Now the impossibility of acquiring these two kinds of knowledge depends upon different factors in each instance. Where we are unable to acquire the universal principles of a science or branch of study, the cause is

---

[1] Compare Aristotle's list of circumstances characterising an action (*Eth.*, iii. 1. 16 ff.) which St. Thomas adopts in i. 2, q. 7, a. 3.

usually (though not universally) a psychological one—a
man has not got ' a head ' for mathematics or astronomy
or logic ;  or as St. Thomas has said, he is not ' aptus natus
scire.' [1] But where the inability is one of acquiring knowledge of particular facts, it is usually due to physical causes
—the relative or absolute inaccessibility of the facts.  If
the wind is in a certain direction you cannot hear a shout ;
if a hedge intervenes you cannot see a man.  Remember-
ing that St. Thomas has identified invincible ignorance with
ignorance which it is impossible to avoid, we observe that
he has implicitly recognised this distinction by giving us
a definition which covers *both* cases, the physical as well
as the psychological.  Had he merely contemplated the
psychological case (as we are at first tempted to suppose
by his method of approach [2]), it would have been enough to
say that invincible ignorance was ' ignorantia eorum quae
quis non aptus natus est scire.'   But that would not have
covered the physical case as well ;  and therefore, after
leading us to think that his definition will be the one just
suggested, he suddenly introduces a new idea by saying
that invincible ignorance is ignorance ' quae studio superari
non potest.'   The test is not to be the kind of incapacity
from which you suffer, but the fact that this incapacity (of
whatever kind it may be) cannot be overcome by diligence.
And this definition, though it first appears in question 76,
has been anticipated as far back as question 6, where antecedent ignorance is only allowed to confer inculpability
after a display of diligence (' diligentia adhibita ').

[1] q. 76, a. 2, *corp.*  By denying (*supra*, p. 29) that any ignorance of
principles which by one's 'state or office' one is bound to know can be inculpable, St. Thomas has apparently denied that there can be any such
psychological impossibility in any given case ;—whatever a man's state or
office may be, he is naturally capable of acquiring the relevant principles.
This however would be absurd ; what St. Thomas has denied is simply
that such ignorance, even though psychologically inevitable, is inculpable.
The man ought to have realised his limitations and resigned his office.

[2] For the only kind of invincible ignorance at which he has hinted
prior to his definition is the psychological kind.

We may now sum up the results which St. Thomas has reached.  Ignorance of anything (whether a general principle or a particular fact) relevant to the immediate consequences of an act in apparent contravention of moral law, excuses from the guilt of sin if the following conditions are satisfied :

1. The act must not be in contravention of any of the first principles of the natural law.

2. Knowledge of the true facts must bring with it regret.

3. The act must have been committed with a clear conscience.

4. The clearness of conscience in the particular case must not be due to any direct or indirect neglect of the agent to keep his conscience alert and free from deadening influences.[1]

5. The ignorance must not be of anything which the agent might be considered morally bound to know by reason either of his ' office ' in general, or of the circumstances in which he finds himself, unless it can be shown that, after the exertion of ' diligence,' the ignorance still remained.  In such a case the ignorance is invincible, and (if the other conditions are satisfied) confers inculpability.

Later discussion kept closely to the principles here laid down, and confined itself to the elucidation of minor difficulties.  St. Thomas, with many others, laboured to establish exactly *what* are the principles of natural law of which no man can be invincibly ignorant.  Others again attempted (with a good deal of success) to evolve a satisfactory test for the ' clearness of conscience ' of which we have spoken.  So Gury,[2] for example, following St.

---

[1] This reminds us once more that the common maxim ' conscientia <certa> semper sequenda,' to which St. Thomas unhesitatingly subscribes, does *not* of necessity carry with it the corollary ' conscientia certa semper excusat.'   Neglect of this caveat produces moral confusion of the most appalling kind ; and it may be alleged that some of Abailard's paradoxes were due to a (possibly wilful) assumption of the interchangeability of the two propositions.

[2] *Compendium Theol. Mor.*, i, § 38.

Alphonso, gives as the answer : ' The confessor should
enquire of the penitent whether he sees anything wrong
(*aliquam indecentiam*) in the act, and whether conscience
suggests that he ought to make further enquiry as to its
legitimacy.' The test seems innocent and obvious enough ;
but when first propounded it caused some heart-burning.
Gabriel Vasquez († 1604) claims to have been the first to
enunciate it ' in nostro collegio Complutensi A.D. 1581 ' ;
and asserts that certain colleagues unnamed took objection
to the doctrine. We can imagine his dismay on learning,
not long after, that these same objectors had plagiarised
without acknowledgment, and were now teaching his
theory as their own. Of the bitter recriminations which
ensued he gives no more than a hint, but no doubt they
followed the lines customary in academic vendettas. The
aggrieved pioneer appears at all events to have had the
last word, for he closes his account with the significant
remark, ' Let this be a lesson to them not to be hasty in
condemning others.' [1]

It was felt, furthermore, that St. Thomas's statement
as to ' diligence ' required amplification. Here rigorist
views tended at times to predominate. As we have already
seen, Alexander of Hales would not allow that Satan's most
ingenious devices could evade detection if the Christian
applied the diligence which the peculiar circumstances of
the case demanded. Jeremy Taylor is no less rigorous.
' In things necessary,' he says, our enquiry must be ' nothing
less than that it be so great and diligent as that the work
be done. . . . In these enquiries we are no otherwise to
make a judgment of our diligence than by the event. What-
soever is less than that is less than duty.' [2] It is only in
things ' not absolutely necessary ' that ' moral diligence '
suffices.[3] But most theologians were content with the

---

[1] Vasquez, *in prim. sec.*, disp. 127, c. 3.
[2] *Duct. Dub.*, bk. iv, c. 1, rule 5 (8).          [3] *Ib.*, rules 9–11.

phrase ' moral diligence ' to cover all cases ; interpreting it,
with another reminiscence of Aristotle, as ' such diligence
as a prudent man would exercise according to the gravity
of the case.' [1]  One modern writer, by no means lax in
his general views, goes out of his way to add that ' supreme
diligence ' is not required ; ' for neither divine nor human
legislators are to be thought of as tyrannical.' [2]

## VI

It may be advisable, before passing from this aspect
of the subject, to add a few words as to the first of the
five Thomist principles we have elicited.  Is there such a
thing as a ' natural moral law ' divinely implanted in every
man's mind in such a way that ' no man can be ignorant of
its first principles ' ?  Doubt has been thrown upon the
assertion by the argument that there is scarcely any moral
' law ' which at some time or another has not been ignored,
and that with a clear conscience, not merely by individuals
but by whole communities.[3]  Duns Scotus could not per-
suade himself that the unity and indissolubility of marriage,
the rights of private property, and so forth were guaranteed
on this authority ; Occam and (to some extent) Gerson
shared his hesitations.[4]  Yet we must admit that in every
society there are certain acts for which the excuse ' I did
not know that it is wrong ' will never be admitted.  We
may not appeal to the ' natural law '; but we do appeal
to the ' conscience of society,' and expect everyone who

---

[1] Tanquerey, Synopsis Theol. Mor., ii. 55, and commonly.  Cf. Vega,
de justif., vi. 18 : Invincible ignorance is ' ea quam vincere non possumus
faciendo omnia quae ad eam vincendam solent et debent probi homines
facere.'

[2] Prümmer, Manuale Theol. Mor., i. 31.

[3] I have alluded to this criticism in Some Principles of Moral Theology,
p. 26.  For further examples see J. Taylor, Duct. Dub., bk. ii, c. 1, rule
1 (46).

[4] Duns Scot., iii Sent. d. 37, q. 1 ; Occam, ii Sent. q. 19, ad dub. 3 ;
Gerson, de vit. spir. an., ii, iii.

is possessed of the use of his reason to be aware of the dictates of that conscience. There are few communities in which, for example, outrageous and inhuman brutality to a child would be condoned on the excuse that no one had told the offender not to do it. We may quarrel with the scholastic mode of statement if we wish, and no doubt it led to much erroneous and dogmatic tabulation of the content of the ' natural law,' and so impeded the free development of thought and institutions. But in one form or another the conception is an anchor and safeguard of corporate life ; and as such every community recognises it in fact, though it may not accept it as a philosophical postulate by name.

In any case, the acceptance and retention of the idea of natural law by the Church had two important consequences. The first need not detain us ; it was simply that the ' natural law ' could always be appealed to, either to justify a revolution, whether in ethical theory or in social organisation, or to vindicate the established order.[1] This made for that fluidity of thought and development which is always desirable as a safety-valve for institutionalism. The second affects our subject directly. In every use of the word ' law ' which custom has sanctioned there is present at least some vestige of the idea of necessity. In so-called ' scientific laws ' or ' physical laws of nature ' necessity is supposed to operate absolutely or automatically ; observed relations are dignified with the name of ' law ' to show that they are contrasted with the ' contingent '—that which might be otherwise and so is unpredictable. The sun cannot refuse to rise ; the ' law ' of gravitation is, within its proper sphere, invariable. But in so far as the subject of any ' law ' is thought of as endowed with a degree of free volition and responsibility, automatism is to a corresponding degree excluded ; and the idea of

[1] *Supra*, pp. 2, 15.

necessity inherent in the term is commonly supplied by the conception of sanctions or penalties which can be put into force to secure obedience. This is true even in cases where neither law nor sanction can be thought of (unless by the most ingenious allegorism) as promulgated by a particular author at a particular point of time. Phrases such as the ' laws of health ' or the ' laws of economics ' combine the conception of an automatic or causal necessity with that of a moral sanction ; the ' law ' is a law both because certain results appear always to be involved in certain causes, and because the results are of such a character as to lead all reasonable men to attempt to avoid them if they are evil, or to embrace them if they are good, by avoiding or putting into operation the causes to which they are commonly attributed. But the influence of the idea of sanctions or penalties is strongest where the law in question is most exclusively concerned with moral ends and actions. In ' civil law ' its dominance is obvious ; and rightly or wrongly it has for centuries held a similar position in relation to both ' the law of the Church ' and ' the law of God.' So the ' law of the Church ' has commonly involved the thought that the Church has the right to impose censures upon those of its members who fail to comply ; and the ' law of God,' that God reserves to Himself the power of punishing neglect of His law either in this world or the next, even if the infringement of the law does not (as in the case of the ' laws of health ') automatically bring its own punitive consequences with it.

But wherever the penal element is to any degree expressed or even latent in laws of any kind affecting human action, the danger of what is commonly called ' formalism ' is always near the surface. Formalism, in effect, is the tendency to obey not out of any respect for the law or for its author, but only through fear of the penalties of disobedience ; and its inevitable corollary is that only such minimum of obedience is given—and that unwillingly, for there is no respect for the law—as will suffice to evade those penalties.[1] That sanctions induce these consequences is not necessarily a reason for condemning them altogether. In many matters the spirit in which an action is performed is of less importance than the fact that it *is* performed ; in comparison with the resultant well-being, it is relatively immaterial whether a man abstains from excess at table through love of health or through fear of indigestion. It may be urged, also, that the enactment of sanctions for offences of a particular kind has an important influence upon the moral education of the subject ;[2] it leads him gradually to the realisation that the offences contemplated must be in themselves serious if they call for such punishment. Furthermore—and it is on these grounds that St. Thomas justifies legislation with sanctions [3]—the unwillingness or formalism may wear off as the action becomes habitual, and the danger of the penal element thus be outweighed by its ultimate efficacy. But in spite of these considerations it is obvious that legislation by sanctions has its dangers, and that the ethical formalism it tends —temporally, at all events—to induce is wholly inadequate to the Christian ideal of virtue.[4]

[1] Aquinas, *S.T.*, i. 2, q. 92, a. 2, obj. 4 : ' qui solo metu poenarum obedit legi non est bonus ' ; Taylor, *Duct. Dub.*, ii. 1, rule 3 : ' To do good out of fear of punishment is to do good no longer than I am observed and no longer than I am constrained.'

[2] So H. Rashdall, *Theory of Good and Evil*, i. 296.

[3] *S.T.*, i. 2, q. 92, a. 1, ad 1. It is further to be noticed that neither Our Lord nor St. Paul, despite their criticism of the law, directs any attack against its penal element. The invective against the Pharisees (Matt. xxiii., etc.) is of course a final condemnation of formalism, but the sanctions which are among its principal occasions are not alluded to. St. Paul bases his criticism of the law upon its inadequacy and its tendency to render attractive what it forbids. Neither Gospels nor Epistles hesitate to accept the existence and legitimacy of spiritual sanctions for the divine law.

[4] This at once raises the question—Must it not therefore be a complete mistake to think of the divine law as equipped with sanctions, and of God as a God who punishes ? By the threat of punishment will He not defeat

It is true that formalism is a danger which may beset
even those who act most upon conscience and least through
fear of external sanctions ; the dictates of conscience can
be elevated into a cast-iron system as burdensome and
tyrannical as any code externally imposed.   Nevertheless it
must be admitted that conflict between the external and
the internal ' norm ' of moral action—between law and

His own end of securing willing acceptance ?   The justification of sanctions
suggested in the text, even though reinforced by the considerations
mentioned in the last footnote, is only a partial reply ;  for it is obvious
that under penal legislation habitual willingness will at best only be slowly
secured ;  and how are we to estimate of the sinner's condition if he dies
before the end is attained ?    He has obeyed the law, it is true, but from the
wrong motive—that of fear—throughout.    St. Thomas discusses this problem in a very interesting passage (S.T., i. 2, q. 100, aa. 9, 10) in which he
asks ' Does the divine law '—which he conceives throughout as operating
by means of sanctions—' demand a virtuous spirit [' modus virtutis,' or
(as in a. 10) ' modus caritatis '—a ' spirit of love '], or only actions formally
correct ? '   To this he is bound to answer in the affirmative—the spirit is
all-important.   He then takes up the problem at the point just indicated :
if the law is penal, will it not operate with crushing rigour against those
who come to be judged before fear of sanctions (or any other motive) has
produced in them the habit of willing obedience ?—' No one can act
virtuously save from the habitude of virtue ;  and therefore anyone who
lacks this habit must deserve punishment ' (or, in a. 10, ' must sin
mortally ') ' in all that he does, however good < both in outward effect and
even in the immediate motive, unless it springs from a habit, > his actions
may be.'   He attempts to avoid this conclusion by suggesting that what
may be called a relative or *ad hoc* willingness to do *this particular act*
for its own sake will satisfy the requirements of the law, even though it
does not spring (as yet) from the ' habit of virtue ' or ' spirit of love.'
Such a state of mind is no doubt psychologically possible.   But St.
Thomas's solution is open to the serious objection that he has not shown
how a penal law can in any particular case produce a willingness to do the
act *for its own sake* ;  and unless it can be shown that the sanctions *do*
produce such willingness (as against the obvious truth that—unless the
willingness is already there—their tendency is to militate against it by
inducing the motive of fear) it must be concluded that his mitigation is
of little value.   It will be almost as difficult to obey the law *ex animo* in all
or most individual cases, as to acquire the *habit* of *ex animo* obedience ;
indeed it might be said that, while sanctions may and at times do produce
this latter result, it is an impossible paradox to suggest that they can *ever*
produce the former.   That being so, a penal law is still of little avail to
the person who has not acquired the habit of virtue—it cannot help him
even to that relative willingness which alone will evade its rigours ; and
the original problem remains as difficult as ever.

conscience—may arise not merely from divergence of guidance given by the two upon particular questions of conduct ; but even more because the penal element inherent in any system of law is bound to promote formalism, whilst conscientiousness is normally (though not always) diametrically opposed to it. The conflict between law and conscience, in other words, is not always or only a conflict as to the letter (' What is the correct action in such and such circumstances ? ') ; but also a conflict of spirit (' With what motive and what zeal is the admittedly correct action to be performed ? ').

The strong bias towards law which Christianity inherited made formalism a very real danger to the Church : its full recognition of the fact and character of conscience gave it an equal recognition of the danger. It was therefore a peculiarly happy circumstance that the Church could recognise one system of law, at least, in which the penal element—and so the danger of formalism—was almost non-existent ; and could invest that system with such dignity that all other systems (even that of the ' positive revealed law ' of God) might be thought of as derived from it, and so as partaking of its character. The ' moral law of nature,' in its strictest sense, is a code without sanctions, embraced for itself alone and not by reason of its consequences. Its content has at all times been inferred from the observation of principles of apparently universal acceptance,[1] despite the diversity of the human codes in which they may have been enshrined. Such principles in their simplest forms are rather assertions of rights than assertions of duty—the right to life, the right to food, the right to shelter, the right to possession ; the idea of sanctions cannot arise until the correlative duty of

---

[1] Isidore Hisp., *Etym.*, v. 4 (quoted *S.T.*, i. 2, q. 95, a. 4, obj. 1) ; though St. Thomas gives it a systematic basis in psychological distinctions (*S.T.*, i. 2, q. 94, a. 2).

respecting the right is taken into account. Again, such penalties as may follow the infringement of a right are exacted either upon the individual initiative of the injured party, or by action on the part of the community or of some of its members ; in either case the sanction for the breach of the natural law must appear to be superadded by human action, and not inherent in the law itself. Similarly God may be supposed to supplement the law of nature by adding sanctions ; there is no *natural* penalty for fratricide, therefore Jahweh imposes the brand of Cain. For all these reasons, no penal element is commonly thought of as attached to the ' law of nature ' ; penalties come in when God repromulgates it as ' revealed,' or man as ' human ' law.[1] It follows that penalties or sanctions are not, in Christian thought, inevitably inherent in the character of law, for all law, divine as well as human, is derived from the law of nature, whose force is independent of sanctions.

[1] So St. Thomas, though he thinks of law in general as having ' coactiva vis ' (i. 2, q. 90, a. 3, ad 2 ; cp. q. 92, a. 2), and regards punishment as in no way contrary to natural law (q. 95, a. 2), says nothing of sanctions in his discussion of the latter, but associates them directly with human and divine law. The natural law thus prescribes ' the acts of virtue ' (q. 94, a. 3) ; but ' perfection of virtue comes only by discipline,' and, for most men (though not for all), such discipline must be imposed ' by force or fear ' (q. 95, a. 1), ' *therefore* it was necessary that<human>laws should be promulgated ' (*ib.*).   So, too, divine law is necessary to provide for the punishment of offences which human law cannot touch (e.g. offences of the spirit) ' that no evil might go unforbidden and unpunished ' (q. 91, a. 4 ; cp. q. 99, a. 6).   Cp. the quotation from Cicero in q. 91, a. 3 : ' initium juris est a naturâ profectum ; deinde quaedam in consuetudinem ex utilitatis ratione venerunt ; postea res a naturâ profectas et consuetudine probatas *legum metus et religio sanxit.*'   Jeremy Taylor (*Duct. Dub.*, ii. 1, rule 3) makes ' fear of punishment ' (i.e. of ' the stings of conscience and the fear of divine vengeance ') the ' first and greatest band of the law of nature.'   But his discussion is marred by a confusion between the ' law of nature ' and the positive divine law, so that it might be thought that sanctions commonly regarded as attached to the latter have as a result been transferred to the former ; and he sometimes waters down this idea of ' fear ' till it is little more than the ' reverence which nature carries in the retinue of all her laws.'   On the whole, however, he misses the opportunity of treating the law of nature as relatively free from the penal element.

Ideally, therefore, all laws, like the law of nature, demand observance for their own sakes ; formalism is in itself a violation of the ideal of law, as well as of the ideal of conscientiousness.

Thus the concept of the ' law of nature ' imported into the Christian system of law an element which made continually for conscientiousness as against formalism. Conscience received an ally of inestimable value in the heart of the enemy's camp.[1] Without such an ally it is possible that the battle would have gone finally against the individual, and the tyranny of authority have become complete. That there were periods when individualism was almost crushed out of existence by ecclesiastical law is of course a commonplace of history ; that no such period was stereotyped into an eternity must be attributed, in part at least, to the fact that the highest and oldest of all laws which the Church recognised was a law without sanctions, respected for itself alone—a law which appealed to conscience and to conscience only, and made formalism impossible. That developing insistence upon the inculpability of con- scientious action, whether technically ' ignorant ' or not, to which the following chapters bear witness, is the happy result of this alliance between the law of nature and the liberty of conscience against the formalist bias of ecclesiastical codes.

For it would be wrong to suppose that we have already reached the extreme limit of the doctrine of invincible ignorance, and that nothing remains to be said on the subject. The dawn of the modern era brought with it events whose far-reaching influence in every direction did not leave even this small corner of theology untouched, but presented the old problems under new and perplexing forms. The first of these events was the discovery of America.

[1] For the relation between the ' law of nature ' and ' conscience ' see *S.T.*, i. 2, q. 94, a. 1, ad 2.

# CHAPTER II

## HEATHEN AND HERETIC

### I

A CURIOUS feature, common to all the discussions of invincible ignorance reviewed in the last chapter, is that whilst two kinds of such ignorance are invariably mentioned, only one of them is seriously considered. Alexander, as we saw, divided ignorance into ignorance *per naturam* and ignorance *ex casu*, and Albert the Great and St. Thomas know of and accept the distinction. The former type implies some defect in the ignorant person ; thus, as Alexander says, there are things which children, the senile, and the mentally deficient cannot be expected to recognise however much diligence be applied. Albert echoes this in his ' moriones et melancholici,' St. Thomas in his ' furiosi et amentes.' [1] But this type of invincible ignorance led to no discussion, and interest was centred on the second kind, ' ignorantia invincibilis ex casu.' Here the ignorance is not natural but accidental—it may be the accident of education or of circumstances—the ignorant person has not been or is not so placed as to know ' what he ought to know.' In most of the definitions of the phrase, this type is the only one recognised. So, for example, Pierrot-Migne, ' Dictionnaire de la Théologie Morale ' (s.v.) : ' Such ignorance is called invincible because one *has not been able* to conquer it completely ' (thus leaving open the question of the future possibility of conquering it). Similarly the ' Catholic Encyclopedia ' : ' Ignorance of which a person *is not able to rid himself* notwithstanding the employment of

[1] *S.T.*, ii. 2, q. 15, a. 1.

moral diligence ' (leaving open the possibility that others—his confessor, for example,—might rid him of it) ; and the ' New English Dictionary ' : ' An ignorance the means of removing which *is not possessed by the ignorant person himself* ' (but not denying that it may be possessed by others).[1]

The type of invincible ignorance commonly contemplated is therefore ignorance which, *at the moment of the action considered*, is actually unconquered ; but which can easily be corrected either on discovery of the true facts of the case, or (if it is an ignorance of some moral or ecclesiastical principle) by a simple statement on the part of a confessor or expert. Most of the cases discussed contemplate, for example, ignorance that such and such an obligation of fasting is laid down by the Church, or that to-day is a day of obligation ; that the beast at which you shoot is really a man, or the enemy whom you strike is really your father.[2] This is genuinely enough ignorance, and, at the moment when the ' sin ' is committed, invincible ' per accidens,' but it is not invincible altogether and in itself. Yet the dominance of this type of problem is further illustrated by the significant practical principle, popular with the casuists, that, sometimes at least, a penitent in invincible ignorance or error ought *not* to be informed of the true facts of the case if it is foreseen that the information will not alter his course of action—*because if he continued in that course after being warned he would no longer be in material but in formal sin.*[3]

---

[1] Cp. Sanderson (*de obl. consc. prael.*, viii. 9), who illustrates invincible ignorance by ' ut si quis aut insania gravi et diuturno morbo laboraverit, aut nuperrime ab externis regionibus reversus fuerit, necquicquam de lege promulgata aut inaudiverit aut audire potuerit.'

[2] See, e.g., Gury, i, §§ 13, 38, sub *Resolves*, and compare the instances already quoted from Abailard and St. Thomas.

[3] Slater, *Manual of Moral Theology*, ii. 223 ; Gury, ii, § 611 ; Taylor, *Duct. Dub.*, bk. i, ch. 3, rule 8. The case usually discussed is one in which an impediment to marriage (not known by the parties) becomes known to the confessor after the marriage has been solemnised. Jeremy Taylor's instance is a very extreme one of this kind. It is needless to add that the principle, unless strictly limited in application, is capable of almost infinite abuse.

There is a certain cynicism about this 'principle' which scarcely commends it, though as a rule of thumb it is not altogether without value. Our purpose in quoting it, however, is simply to illustrate the contention that 'invincible ignorance,' in the common usage of moralists, means no more than lack of information which, at the moment and in the circumstances contemplated, is not actually available for the agent's use.

Such ignorance is *merely temporarily* invincible ;—not necessarily 'unconquerable' in any full sense of the word. On the other hand, the cases covered by Alexander of Hales's first category of 'ignorance invincible by nature' imply something which is genuinely and completely unconquerable, but not necessarily ignorance in the strict sense at all. For the child, or old man, or mentally defective, so long as he remains what he is, cannot be expected to have any further understanding of the principle of which he is 'invincibly ignorant,' *though he may be able to repeat the words or formula in which that principle is enshrined.* A child can recite the decalogue without any comprehension of its meaning ; in such a case he is, at all events for the time being, no better and no worse off than his playfellow to whom it is wholly unknown. The mere question as to whether he is ignorant of the principle as expressed in a form of words is entirely indifferent ; what makes his breach of it (if he breaks it) blameless, is want of comprehension or acceptance. So that the invincible ignorance which confers inculpability in this case is really invincible *stupidity* [1] or invincible *incredulity*— it may coexist in fact with a verbal knowledge of the principle concerned. The criterion of ignorance is no longer 'lack of information,' but rather 'inability to comprehend or to conform.'

[1] So in the case, previously mentioned as discussed by Alexander, of the cleric who cannot commit to memory his canon law. He cannot be called *ignorant* of it—in any strict sense of the word ; and yet he certainly does not *know* it. (*Supra*, p. 20.)

This opens up a wide question. Between Alexander's two extremes lies a whole range of other mental states which partake in varying degree of the nature of both. They are states of what we may call 'conscientious incredulity' towards certain known principles or dogmas, which yet seem to deserve the title of 'invincible' because they do not result from any lack of moral diligence. We may instance the case of the Christian who in all good conscience, and with real regret that he differs from the Church to which he belongs, is unable to bring himself to accept, let us say, the doctrine of the Real Presence or the practice of auricular confession, though he has used every effort to set them before himself in a favourable light. Is this invincible ignorance? Ignorance in the strict sense it is not, for the questioner *knows* the formulated doctrine; but does his condition approximate to that of those who are invincibly ignorant 'per naturam'—is he, according to the general tradition of moral theology, free from blame? [1]

It is not surprising that this question does not meet us to any extent in the Schoolmen. It is admitted on all hands that heathen 'qui nihil audierunt de fide' are not *on that account* to be considered sinners,[2] in spite of Augustine's

---

[1] That such an extension of the strict meaning of 'ignorance' would not be foreign to mediæval thought is clear from the following passages of Hugh St. Victor :—*Annot. eluc. in ep. ad Rom.*, i. : 'non intelligere aliquando dicitur ignorare ; aliquando in memoria non habere ; aliquando quod in memoria est opere non implere ; aliquando non approbare ; *eodem modo et nescire.*' Cp. Id., *in ep. prim. ad Cor.* : 'ignorantia alia ex contemptu, alia ex infirmitate, alia ex defectu rationis.' So, too, Aquinas (*S.T.*, i. 2, q. 76, a. 4, ad 3) admits 'non recognoscere' as an occasionally justifiable interpretation of 'ignorantia.'

[2] Aquinas, *S.T.*, ii. 2, q. 10, a. 1, in corp. ; *de verit.*, xiv. 11, ad 1 ; cp. Abailard, *Scito Teipsum*, 13 ; *Errores M. Baii damn. a Pio V*, October 1597, no. 68 (Denz.-Bann., 1068) ; de Lugo, *de virt. fid. div.*, xix. 10, 18 ff. (where the principal references are given). Suarez, *de fid. theol.*, xvii. 1, n. 5, gives other references ; *ib.*, nn. 2, 11, opinions to the contrary. The doctrine is most fully expressed in Pius IX, *Encycl.*, 'Quanto conficiamur moerore' (August 10, 1863 ; Denz.-Bann., 1677 ; *infra*, p. 62), which indeed refers not merely to the heathen but to heretics in good faith as well. See also Billot, 'La Providence de Dieu,' in *Études* (November 20,

hesitation to which reference has already been made. But —once this class of 'infidel' had been set on one side—it must have been extremely difficult for the mediæval mind to conceive it possible that anyone should be aware of a particular precept or dogma as a precept or dogma of the Church, and yet be conscientiously unable to accept it as binding upon himself. Such an attitude would be tantamount to a pertinacious rejection of the faith, and so to wilful infidelity. The lesser sin, the failure to obey the precept or the doubt as to the dogma, would be swallowed up in the greater, that of contumacy against the Church. In practice, for those who held the authority of ecclesiastically promulgated or accepted laws to be finally binding in conscience, the excuse of invincible ignorance, in the normal sense of the phrase, could only be urged in defence of a breach of the law where the ignorance was of a purely accidental kind—where the sinner *did not know* of the law or doctrine or *did not know* that a particular law should have governed his action.

Cases of conscientious inability to believe a doctrine propounded by the Church as true, or to obey a precept propounded as obligatory, would at best be regarded, therefore, as only theoretically possible under such a system. On this account mediæval moralists thunder against infidels, heretics, schismatics and apostates,[1] without the slightest recognition of the possibility that these misguided individuals may after all be following the stringent dictates of

1921), on the various forms in which the doctrine has been held ; and *ib.* (September 5, 1922) for instances of its denial. Cardinal Billot's important series of articles is to discuss the whole question of the salvability of heretics ; this part of it, however, has unfortunately not appeared so far.

[1] Thus Hinckmar of Rheims, *de praedest.*, 24 ; Aquinas, *S.T.*, ii. 2, q. 11, *pass.*—especially a. 2, ad 3—as soon as a proposition has been defined by the authority of the universal Church, to resist it is heresy and (consequently) sin ; *ib.*, a. 3, in corp. and ad 3. Cp. especially the Fourth Lateran Council, c. 3 (Mirbt, *Quellen zur Geschichte des Papsttums*, 278) ; Council of Florence, *Decret. pro Jacob.* (Denz.-Bann., 714).

conscience; and they have no word of sympathy for any form of doubt.[1]  The case of the man who conscientiously finds himself unable to accept a known precept of the Church as binding is wholly ignored.  Conscientious doubt, whether in faith or morals, seems at first sight to be beyond the purview of the Catholic moral code.

## II

Further consideration, however, shows this conclusion to be very far from true.  While it is clear that mediæval moralists ignore the possibility of a knowing yet conscientious (as distinct from a merely ignorant) divergence from the Church in matters of faith or conduct, their post-Reformation successors look on the problem with far kinder eyes.  The sixteenth century presented Catholicism with two fresh problems.  The first was that of innumerable heathen in the New World on whom the preaching of the gospel made little or no impression; the second, that of baptised and professing Christians who, by the accident of birth and education, were so inured to heresy that they could not grasp the true faith even when it was put before them.  In the solution of these problems the Church found a new use for the old category of invincible ignorance.  The plea which had never hitherto been urged on behalf of dissentients is now accepted in their defence;  and even those *who have heard of the faith and yet are conscientiously unable to accept it* are allowed the benefit of the doubt—they may be free from guilt on the score of invincible ignorance.  Here ' invincible ' is used in the full sense of ' morally insuperable,' and ' ignorance ' shades off into the wider meanings of ' incredulity ' or ' nonconformity.'  There is something about the conscience of many brought up in heathen and heretical

---

[1] Note the very cold references to *dubitatio infidelitatis* and *incredulitatis* in Aquinas, *S.T.*, 3, q. 27, a. 4, ad 2.

E

surroundings which makes it morally impossible for them, even after hearing *about* the true faith, to accept it. Infidelity is of course always 'material' sin, but often enough along this line it may be thought of as coming from an invincibly erroneous conscience, and so free from all guilt of 'formal' sin.

The new way of thought developed with startling suddenness. The Schoolmen, it would appear, though well acquainted with Jews and 'Saracens,' had little conception of a heathen world in gross. Even those who hesitated to accept the dogmatic belief of some of the Fathers, that the world had been completely evangelised in apostolic times,[1] thought of the infidel merely as an occasional individual who through accident of time and geography had missed the proclamation of the gospel. To St. Thomas he is simply 'an uncultured man,' 'brought up amidst woods and wolves'[2]—a freak of nature in an otherwise evangelised universe. That amazing encyclopedia of ethics and canon law, the 'Summa Summarum Sylvestrina,' which—like an index—appropriately closes mediæval thought on these subjects, gives no hint of the surprise to come. The articles 'infidelitas,' 'haeresis,' 'ignorantia' reproduce the scholastic commonplaces in a merely formal way. Sylvester completed the 'Summa' before 1516, and died in 1523. With a writer only twenty years his junior, Francis à Victoria († 1546), we find ourselves transported to an utterly new age and atmosphere.

Victoria, a Dominican professor at Salamanca, was a man of exceptional genius. Among his admiring and grateful

[1] So Chrysostom and others on Matt. xxiv. 14.

[2] *de veritate*, xiv. 11 ; *in Rom.*, x. 3 ; Cardinal Billot, 'La Providence de Dieu,' in *Études*, November 1921 and September 1922. Fr. Harent (Vacant et Mangenot, *Dictionnaire de Théol. Cath.*, vii., 1897, 1898) disputes Billot's view that the recognition of heathendom was so slight in the thirteenth century, but only succeeds in proving that a wide *geographical* knowledge was current in some circles. The whole tone of the scholastic discussions supports the Cardinal.

pupils occur the names of Melchior Cano, Dominic Soto, and Bartholomew à Medina, the reputed parent of probabilism. Like other great teachers he could not be induced to publish his lectures ; such of them as survive were given to the world posthumously.[1] Among them a volume of ' Relectiones Theologicae' became famous by reason of two short essays ' de Indis '—a subject ' undertaken,' he tells us, ' on account of those barbarians of the New World, commonly called Indians, who came under Spanish dominion forty years ago, though previously they were unknown.' ' Propter barbaros istos ' he puts the question, Is imperialism Christian ?—Have we any right to the territory of the Indians ? Victoria himself believed that he was the first ever to broach the subject : ' notandum quod ego nihil vidi scriptum de hac quaestione, nec unquam interfui disputationi aut consilio de hac materia.'[2] He is not even certain upon what ground the imperialist will take his stand (i. § 40) ; but as best he can he marshals the arguments. Some of them are scholastic—the Emperor is ruler of the whole world ; the Pope makes the same claim ; either can ' grant ' the lands of the barbarian to the conqueror (§§ 24–30). Nay, the lands never belonged to the barbarian at all ; he is in mortal sin, he has resisted the preaching of the gospel, therefore his claim is forfeit (§§ 5, 31). But others have a wholly modern sound ; the matter is after all *fait accompli,* why discuss it ?—undeveloped lands (' deserta ') belong by

---

[1] Quétif et Echard, *Script. Ord. Praed.,* ii. 130. Victoria is better known to-day as a jurist than as a theologian. The Carnegie Endowment for Universal Peace has recently published a critical text of the *de Indis,* with an important introduction by E. Nys, and translation and facsimiles (Oxford, 1917). There is also a valuable estimate of Victoria, as a precursor of Grotius in the systematising of the idea of international law, with a full and accurate analysis of the *de Indis,* in T. A. Walker, *History of the Law of Nations* (Cambridge, 1899), pp. 214 ff.

[2] There are, however, here and there reminiscences of the classical discussion in Augustine (*de civ. Dei,* iii. 10 ; iv. 3, 6, 15) ; and his formulation of the causes of a ' just war ' owes a good deal to the Schoolmen.

natural and international law to their discoverers;—the barbarians freely chose Spanish rule (he draws a striking picture of the trembling and unarmed natives ' electing ' for the Spanish king within a cordon of his troops) ;—it is the ' gift of God '—the white man's burden, in fact (§§ 3, 31, 40). All these suggestions Victoria refutes without difficulty, but with a clear and Christian insight into their fallacies, in the first essay ; in the second, whither—in spite of its interest and importance—we need not follow him, he builds up a theory of his own which, it must be confessed, leaves the imperialist with small grounds for complacency.

What, however, especially impressed his successors was his striking defence of the possibility of the heathen rejecting the gospel without sin. True, they are bound to listen to a missionary who comes peaceably and earnestly bespeaks their attention (§ 36) ; ' and if the Christian faith is put before them "probabiliter," that is with probable and reasonable arguments, with a virtuous life studiously in accord with the law of nature . . . if this be done not once only or perfunctorily, but diligently and studiously, *then* they are bound to receive it under pain of mortal sin ' (§ 37). But the mere proclamation of the gospel is not enough ' sine miraculis aut quacumque alia probatione aut suasione ' (§ 34), and he adds, rather sadly, ' I am not clear that Christianity has been preached and put before the barbarians hitherto in such a fashion as that they are bound to believe it under pain of sin. . . . I hear of no miracles, nor examples of specially religious conduct ; nay rather, of many scandals, of fierce outrages, of many impieties. So it would seem that Christianity has *not* been preached to them in the appropriate and godly way (' satis commode et pie '), though many regulars and seculars no doubt have brought to the task, by life and example and devotion to preaching, a diligence which would have been sufficient had not others, whose hearts are set elsewhere (' quibus alia est cura '), stood in the way ' (§ 38).  Where the barbarians, in such circumstances, have refused to believe, they are excused from sin ; and though they *have heard* the gospel message their state may still approximate to one of invincible ignorance (§§ 33–35).

The novelty of this teaching lies in the fact that ignorance is no longer thought of as bare absence of knowledge, but as an inability to accept Catholic truth.  Two reasons may be alleged for such an unfortunate state of affairs where it arises.  The first may be the failure of the missionary to adjust himself to the needs of his hearers—his proposition of the faith is, in the circumstances in which he preaches it, ' insufficient.'  This was the point seized upon by Victoria. But while such a theory is very salutary for the missionary, it is too simple to  fit all the facts.  There is a second cause at work.  Part at least of the deadlock must arise from the state of the hearer's mind, his previous education, or his present environment, which seem to make diligence on his part and on that of the missionary equally ineffective.  It is misleading to call this state one of ' ignorance ' ; and it is not clear why the old phrase was used in this new connection.  But it had at least this much appropriateness, that the tests which had been found satisfactory in the earlier case appeared equally appropriate in the new.  Where the heathen, in all good conscience, after the use of moral diligence, and with genuine regret, is unable to accept the Christian faith and rule of life, surely he must be regarded as inculpable ?


### III

It may be hazarded at once that this new development would not have commended itself to St. Thomas.  He had not, it is true, the same urgent reasons for considering it ; and the rarity of the heathen, so far as he was concerned, made it possible for him, as will appear, to adopt another theory about them. But he was perfectly cognisant with the type of man who could not accept the faith ; and he had a place ready for him in his system. His authorities had acquainted him with two psychological states to which the names of ' caecitas mentis ' and ' hebetudo sensus ' [1] were given. St. Thomas could quite easily have treated these two psychological states as arising ' ex natura,' and have seen in them insuperable (and therefore inculpable) obstacles to acceptance of the faith. Thereby he would have left room in his system for ' invincible ignorance ' of the special type contemplated by Victoria—the state of mind of those who have heard the faith but cannot accept it. But so far is he from doing this, that he insists (in the face of strong arguments to the contrary) that ' blindness of mind ' and ' dulness of apprehension ' are *sins*, and not merely psychological conditions for which the person concerned has no responsibility. Further, to make assurance doubly sure, he so fits them into his system as to avoid all possibility of treating them as excuses for infidelity. A man can be as blind of mind and as dull of apprehension as you wish ; but it need not for a moment interfere with his lively acceptance of the faith.

We must postpone to a later chapter the problem raised by these facts. It is indeed an important problem—why should St. Thomas have been so anxious to make any and every kind of conscious departure from the faith a culpable offence ? All that need be said at the moment is that tradition scarcely accounts for his zeal. It is true that Gregory numbered both ' caecitas ' and ' hebetudo ' among the enemies whom the celestial war-horse (the simile by which, at the moment, the Christian is represented) has to meet ; and assigned each to its proper family among the seven capital sins. ' Blindness ' is placed among the children of lust, ' dulness ' among

---

[1] Gregory, *Moralia*, xxxi. 45 (88).

those of gluttony. But the artifices of mediæval reinter-
pretation would have been equal to the situation had St.
Thomas wished to make ' blindness ' and ' dulness ' excuses
for infidelity. The fact is, however, that he did not wish to
do anything of the kind.

So he boldly faces the arguments brought forward to
exempt ' blindness of mind ' from culpability.[1] They are
not unimportant, for they are based upon good scriptural
and traditional grounds. There is first of all the word of
Christ (John ix. 41), ' If ye had been blind ye would not have
had sin,' which implies the inculpability of acts arising from
this mental condition, and by analogy (' Neither did he sin,
nor his parents ') the inculpability of the condition itself.
There are, again, Old Testament passages (Isa. vi. 10 is
quoted as the objector's instance) which make spiritual
blindness an affliction coming from God ; this cannot be
' culpa ' or ' peccatum '—at most it is ' poena.' Further,
Augustine has said that all sin is voluntary ; [2] but few if
any blind themselves voluntarily ; how then is blindness
sin ? St. Thomas gives ground a little before these arguments. There *is* a blindness which comes ' ex naturali
defectu non potentis videre,' and this excuses from sin. There
is also a blindness which comes from God, and this is punishment and not sin. But having made these admissions, he
counter-attacks vigorously. The first kind of blindness
occurs, after all, only when the mind is deficient in its
natural equipment, ' sicut patet in amentibus et furiosis ' ;
and idiots and madmen are not fit subjects for ethical
judgments. The second kind comes indeed from God, but
it is a punishment for sin, and therefore the man himself is
responsible, ' wherefore it is said of some, *Their wickedness
hath blinded them.*' [3] In neither case, therefore, will he admit
any excuse for the normal man on this count.

1 *S.T.*, ii. 2, q. 15, a. 1.      2 *de ver. rel.*, 14.
3 Wisd. ii. 21.

But further, the third (and, as he insinuates, the most ordinary) form of spiritual blindness is one for which man is wholly responsible. ' The third source of mental vision is the " intelligible principle "' (may we fairly translate this as the ' mental picture ' ?) ' to which a man can attend or not as he will. When he fails to attend to it, it is either because he deliberately withholds from considering it (as in Ps. xxxvi. 3, *He would not understand to do good*) ; or because his mind is occupied with other things which he loves more (as in Ps. lviii. 8, *The fire fell, and they could not see the sun*[1]). And either of these kinds of mental blindness is sin.'

There follows a short and unnecessary discussion of the difference (if any) between ' blindness ' and ' dulness,' in which nothing important emerges except the further admission that ' dulness, like blindness of mind, is sinful *in so far as it is voluntary* ; as is clear in the case of the man who has a distaste for (' fastidit ') subtle discussions of spiritual things, or neglects them, because he is wrapped up in carnal things.'[2]   Then, in the third article of this ' quaestio,' St. Thomas has to attend to the objection of those who ask, ' If these mental conditions are such that a man is responsible for them, from what sins do they arise? '   Gregory had attributed them to a carnal origin, but many carnally-minded men have been singularly subtle in abstract discussion. The point is not important, and St. Thomas has little difficulty in showing that carnal-mindedness in the long run will cause spiritual dulness. But this is a long way from proving that ' blindness ' and ' dulness ' are always sins for which a man is responsible ; indeed—though St. Thomas set out to prove it—the admissions he has made go far to show that he really

---

[1] ' Supercecidit ignis et non viderunt solem.'   The English version (verse 7 in P.B. ; 8 in A.V. and R.V.) renders quite differently.   St. Thomas explains ' ignis ' as ' scilicet concupiscentiae.'

[2] *S.T.*, ii. 2, q. 15, a. 2.

recognised a large number of cases in which these states were involuntary and so inculpable.

Faith is that one of the theological virtues which primarily concerns the mind, and ' blindness ' and ' dulness ' are mental defects.[1] Nothing could be more natural, therefore, than to set them down with infidelity as ' sins against faith.' The fact that St. Thomas is careful not to do this requires an explanation ; and the most probable one is that, having made so many admissions as to the possibility of their involuntariness, he dare not oppose them to faith—for that would result in the inconvenient conclusion that faithlessness, among those who had heard the faith, might often be inculpable. Luckily for him, his elastic system could find a place for them elsewhere. His whole formulation of virtues and vices suffered from an embarrassment of riches in the form of traditional material ; the acuteness and ingenuity of psychological analysis which he displays throughout this second part of the 'Summa' are due, at least in some measure, to the need for finding a particular aspect of the soul's activity to correspond to each of the traditional terms of which he knew so many. On the side of goodness of character he had to allow not merely for four cardinal and three theological virtues, but for seven gifts of the Spirit,[2] seven beatitudes,[3] and twelve fruits of the Spirit ; [4] not to speak of the additional embarrassment caused by the ' hundredfold and sixtyfold and thirtyfold ' of Matt. xiii. 23.[5] It is a liberal education in scholastic method to watch him fitting all these heterogeneous elements into one scheme (not without some hesitations and corrections by the way), and then balancing the account, item by item, from an equally heterogeneous list of sins. And in the process of this *tour de force* of

[1] Of ' caecitas mentis ' this is obvious. Of ' hebetudo sensus ' St. Thomas asserts it (following Gregory), *S.T.*, ii. 2, q. 15, a. 2.
[2] *Ib.* i. 2, q. 68.                    [3] *Ib.* q. 69.
[4] *Ib.* q. 70.                              [5] *Ib.* a. 3, ad 2.

pedantry, as has been suggested, psychological distinctions of real value and acuteness continually emerge.

The ' gifts of the Spirit ' (Isa. xi. 2), which St. Gregory had used as the spiritual interpretation of Job's seven sons, are introduced by St. Thomas as special graces ' added ' by God to the virtues, to dispose men to even ' higher activities ' of saintliness.[1] The theological and cardinal virtues ' do not so far dispose a man towards his ultimate end that he does not constantly require to be moved by some higher inspiration of the Holy Spirit.'[2] There is some difficulty, however, in allocating these ' gifts.' There are seven virtues and seven ' gifts ' ; to pair them off would seem the obvious course. But there are three intellectual ' gifts ' (' intellect,' ' science,' and ' wisdom '); and only one intellectual virtue (' faith '). Faith therefore in the end receives two of the intellectual gifts (the third—' wisdom ' —going for special reasons to ' charity ') ; and temperance is left without a gift.[3] This makes it quite feasible for St. Thomas to regard not only ' blindness ' and ' dulness,' but even ignorance as well, as ' sins ' opposed not to faith, but to the gifts of ' intellect ' and ' science ' which ' correspond ' to faith ; and so he does. On this basis he might even have taken the extreme step of denying that ignorance itself, however inculpable, could in any case be an excuse for want of faith ; but here no doubt common sense and a respect for tradition stopped him. What is quite clear is that ' blindness ' and ' dulness,' being now opposed not to faith but only to a ' gift,' can never impede the activity of faith ; and therefore even though, as his objectors suggest, they may be themselves inculpable, they can never make absence of faith inculpable too.

However much St. Thomas would have disapproved

---

[1] S.T., i. 2, q. 68, a. 1.          [2] Ib. a. 2, ad 2.
[3] On this see W. H. V. Reade, *Moral System of Dante's Inferno*, pp. 171–173.

of any theory which made conscientious rejection of
the gospel by the heathen inculpable, the curious fact
remains that he himself had made that development
possible. In shifting the centre of interest from the
character of the ignorance involved in invincible
ignorance, to the conscientiousness or otherwise of the
agent, he had moralised the problem beyond recognition.
From that moment the question of ignorance or knowledge
ceased to be of particular importance ; the inculpability
of the agent was established or denied according as his
conscience was found to be clear or guilty. St. Thomas
in fact had taken problems of ignorance out of the
atmosphere of a court of law into that of the moral judgment. It must seem strange therefore that he should so
readily stamp ' caecitas mentis ' and ' hebetudo sensus '
as sins, and as sins which, even if inculpable, could not
impede the act of faith ; and to this problem we must
return. All that Victoria did was to apply the test of
conscientiousness to the new type of case, as St. Thomas
had done to the old. If the man who had never heard the
creed was blameless, so, it seemed to him, must the man
be also, who having heard it was in all good conscience
unable to accept it.

IV

The logic of the situation soon carried the doctrine
further. If the heathen who had heard the faith and
refused it might be adjudged blameless, the same must be
true of the heretic born and bred—baptised a Christian,
though in circumstances which made him deaf to the
appeal of Catholicism. Hitherto ' pertinacity ' had been
the distinguishing mark of heresy ; [1] now conscientious
pertinacity must be exempt. So Vasquez [2] attacks Castro's

---

[1] So Aug., *Ep.* 162 ; *de civ. Dei*, xviii. 51 ; Aquinas, *S.T.*, ii. 2, q. 2,
a. 6, etc.

[2] *in prim. sec.*, disp. 127, c. 3.

opinion [1] that ' he who, after due warning, refuses to abandon his error, is a heretic ' ; and holds, on the contrary, ' Such a refusal, even though the warning be given by men of the utmost weight (' gravissimi viri '), does not constitute contumacy (and so heresy), so long as the person concerned firmly believes that his doctrine is not opposed to that of the whole Church, and holds those weighty men to be wrong.' Suarez († 1617), on the other hand, though he credits with invincible ignorance ' those who have heard something of the Christian faith, by rumour or report or some kind of insufficient preaching,' [2] is more guarded. He agrees (with some minor reservations) with those who hold that a mere statement of the Catholic doctrine by a ' bishop or inquisitor' is ' sufficient' teaching, and that after such a statement there can be no further excuse for the now enlightened suspect.[3] Cardinal de Lugo [4] († 1660) is much more explicit. For him, as for Suarez, invincible ignorance is ' eorum quibus auctoritas Catholicae ecclesiae numquam fuit sufficienter proposita.' [5] But on the question whether monition by a bishop or inquisitor removes all excusable insufficiency of knowledge, while admitting that it should probably be considered to do so in the case of an uneducated man, he is quite clear that for an instructed theologian with conscientious difficulties it may not be sufficient to overcome his invincible ignorance.[6]

[1] Which had the solid support of Augustine (de gest. Pel., 6 (18) ; de bapt. c. Don., iv. 6 (23) ) and Aquinas (S.T., ii. 2, q. 11, a. 2).

[2] de fid. theol., xvii. 1, nn. 6, 9 ; cp. xv. 2, n. 5, and xix. 5, n. 1.

[3] ib., xix. 3, nn. 20, 21. His principal reservation is that the official in question must make it clear that he is declaring the opinion of the infallible Church. This in itself marks a limitation of an earlier and more rigorous point of view.

[4] On him see F. Heiler, Katholizismus, 612 ; F. von Hügel, Essays and Addresses, 63, 252 ; but note that the passage ostensibly quoted from de Lugo by Heiler is merely von Hügel's summary of his teaching ; and that the German writer reproduces (from another page of von Hügel) references to de Lugo, one of which is incorrect and neither very apposite.

[5] de virt. fid. div., xx, n. 194.

[6] ib., xx, n. 162.

He has even distinct qualms on the subject of the death
penalty for heresy; while asserting the Church's right to
demand it he points out that the method has only been
adopted after all other expedients have failed. Suarez—
with Bellarmine and other controversialists of the period—
had few if any qualms of this kind; and de Lugo explicitly condemns some of his opinions on the whole subject
as 'too rigorous.'[1] A similar contrast between the rigorist
and the liberal outlook may be noticed in contemporary
Anglicanism. Bishop Sanderson is unwilling to admit
that a Roman Catholic in England has any excuse for his
contumacy : 'Thou livest as in a Goshen, where the light
encompasseth thee in on all sides, where there are burning
and shining lamps in every corner of the land. Yet is thy
blindness greater and more inexcusable.'[2] Jeremy Taylor,
on the other hand, says simply : 'Invincible ignorance
. . . is of things which we cannot know because we have
never heard of them, and' (but ought it not to be 'or'?)
'*are not taught sufficiently.*'[3]

It is true no doubt that the old intolerant spirit lived
on ;[4] but the application of the doctrine of invincible
ignorance to the problem of heresy established itself firmly.
Thus Alphonso Liguori could say ' So long as a heretic holds
his own sect to be more worthy of belief than, or as worthy
of belief as <the Catholic Church>, he is not bound to believe
<in the Catholic Church>, because the faith has not been
put before him sufficiently; and it would be imprudent of
him to do so ';[5] and quotes Sanchez († 1610) and Laymann
(† 1635) in support. Pius IX opened a wide field to the
excuse of invincible ignorance for heretics in the following
words : ' It must be regarded as certain that those who

---

[1] *de virt. fid. div.*, xxiv. 2, *pass.* ; cp. Suarez, *op. cit.*, xxiii. 2, n. 16.
[2] *Sermo* vi. *ad pop.*, § 19.    [3] *Duct. Dub.*, bk. iv, ch. 1, rule 5 (12).
[4] For examples see Heiler, *Katholizismus*, 322, 325 ; Hastings, *Encyclopedia of Religion and Ethics*, s.v. ' Persecution (Modern Christian) '; etc.
[5] *Theol. Mor.*, lib. 2, tract. 1, c. 2 (9).

labour under invincible ignorance of the true religion are not thereby adjudged guilty before the eyes of God.  But who would be so bold as to lay down the limits of such ignorance, in face of the variations of character exhibited by races, climates, dispositions and a thousand other influences ? ' [1] Again, in an encyclical to the bishops of Italy, he writes : ' I cannot but allude in condemnation to a grave error, held (I regret to say) by some Catholics, who think that those who live in error, and separate from the true faith and Catholic unity, may attain everlasting life.  Such a doctrine is profoundly uncatholic.  We recognise of course that those who labour under invincible ignorance of our most holy faith, and keep the natural law and its precepts, which God has graven upon every heart,— who are willing to obey God, and live an honourable and upright life—*can*, by the power of the divine light and grace, attain eternal life.  God, who sees and knows the mind, the soul, the heart, the dispositions of every man, would scarcely in His mercy allow anyone to suffer eternal torment unless he were guilty of voluntary sin.' [2]

[1] ' Pro certo habendum est, qui verae religionis ignorantia laborant, si ea sit invincibilis, nulla ipsos obstringi hujusce rei culpa ante oculos Domini.  *Nunc vero quis tantum sibi arroget, ut hujusmodi ignorantiae designare limites queat juxta populorum, regionum, ingeniorum, aliarumque rerum tam multarum rationem et varietatem ?* ' (*Allocutio*, December 9, 1854 ; Mirbt, 349 ; Denz.-Bann., 1647).  The reference to the variations of races, regions, dispositions, etc., would be pointless unless ' invincible ignorance ' in the later sense were intended.

[2] ' Commemorare et reprehendere opportet gravissimum errorem in quo nonnulli catholici misere versantur, qui homines in erroribus viventes et a vera fide atque a catholica unitate alienos ad aeternam vitam pervenire posse opinantur.  Quod quidem catholicae doctrinae vel maxime adversatur.  Notum Nobis vobisque est, eos, qui invincibili circa sanctissimam nostram religionem ignorantia laborant, quique naturalem legem ejusque praecepta in omnium cordibus a Deo insculpta sedulo servantes ac Deo oboedire parati honestam rectamque vitam agunt, posse, divinae lucis et gratiae operante virtute, aeternam consequi vitam ; cum Deus qui omnium mentes, animos, cogitationes habitusque plane intuetur, scrutatur et noscit, pro summa sua bonitate et clementia minime patiatur quempiam aeternis puniri suppliciis qui voluntariae culpae reatum non habeat.' (*Encyclical* ' Quanto conficiamur moerore,' August 10, 1863 ; Denz.-Bann., 1677).  The first sentence quoted obviously rules out any theory of salvation by ' fides late dicta ' (*infra*, pp. 71 ff. ; and cp. the Syllabus

The doctrine is now a commonplace. So Pesch says : ' There must be sufficient certainty before faith can be expected or its absence blamed ' ;[1] and Tanquerey, ' Material or involuntary heresy is that which proceeds from ignorance without pertinacity of will. It exists where a man is ready to submit himself to the authority of God as the revealer and to the infallible judgment of the Church, *so soon as he knows that such truth has been divinely revealed.* Many Protestants and schismatics born in heresy and schism are material heretics : they have never conceived any serious doubts as to the truth of their religion because the faith has either never been put before them at all, *or has been put before them insufficiently.'* [2]

Time has almost, if not quite, avenged Abailard. Not all the positions for which he contended were granted by Christendom. Some indeed can never be, so long as it is agreed that there can be no excuse of invincible ignorance for breaches of the law of nature. Yet the content of the doctrine which was first elaborated as a defence against his antinomianism was not exhausted ; and under stress of the problems raised by the discovery of America it was to be carried to lengths which would have filled even his liberal mind with horror. Invincible ignorance had so far availed for the inculpability of the conscientious heathen, whether they had heard the gospel or no ; it remained to consider its bearing upon the much more serious problem of their salvation.

(1864), nos. 15–17 (Denz.-Bann., 1715–1717)) ; but it is not clear *which* theory as to the salvability of the virtuous heathen (see next chapter) is favoured by the remainder of the quotation.

[1] *Theol. Dogm.*, i. 83 ; iii. 246–253.

[2] *Synopsis Theol. Mor.*, i. 379 ; cp. Billot, *de virt. infus.*, i. 353. It is to be noticed that Gury, who usually follows Liguori closely, omits all reference to this test of ' sufficiency.' He defines a ' material heretic ' merely as ' one who is ready to submit to the judgment of the Church when he recognises his error ; who knows nothing of the true faith and has never doubted his own religion ; and who, when he begins to doubt, applies himself to discover the truth as much as he can ' (*Compend.*, i, § 210).

# CHAPTER III

## FAITH AND SALVATION

### I

THE problem which occupied us in the last chapter was this : How far is the heathen, or heretic born-and-bred, who in good faith and after careful consideration cannot see his way to accept the Christian revelation, inculpable and free from the guilt of infidelity ? To this it has generally been replied that, provided his inability to comply with the rule of faith and life propounded to him satisfies the general principles governing the inculpability of invincible ignorance, his case comes under the same category, which for this purpose is understood in a more extended sense than was usual in mediæval times. This, however, is at best cold comfort to the virtuous heathen and his friends. It assures him of blamelessness *in this particular matter*, but it does not assure him of salvation. Indeed, as far as salvation is concerned, he stands where he did.[1] Three great barriers loom between him and any hope of heaven. One is the traditional principle ' nulla salus extra ecclesiam ' ;[2] though that at least can be mitigated by an extension of the idea of the Church. The second is the doctrine that original sin (with which no one can enter heaven) can only be washed

---

[1] Cp. Suarez, *de fid. theol.*, xii. 3.
[2] For extreme expressions of it see Cyprian, *de unit.*, 6 ; Lactantius, *Div. inst.*, iv. 30. 11 ; Jerome, *Ep.* 15, 2 ; Aug., *Serm. ad Caes. eccl.*, 6 ; Fulgentius, *de fide ad Petrum*, 2 (22), 38 (79).

away by baptism ; [1] this too is made less terrible by admitting the possibility of spiritual substitutes for the rite. But the third is the dominical word : ' He that believeth not shall be damned ' ; [2] and that to the mediæval mind was final. And even if the Schoolmen had been privileged to know that the final verses of the Second Gospel were undoubtedly spurious, they would still have stumbled (as indeed they did) over Hebrews xi. 6 : ' Sine fide autem impossibile est placere Deo ; credere enim opportet accedentem ad Deum quia est, et inquirentibus se remunerator sit '; or Romans xiv. 23 : ' Omne quod non est ex fide, peccatum est.' But how could the heathen believe in Him of whom they had not heard ? And how could they hear without a preacher ? And since (as Soto and Vega were careful to point out [3]) there was no evidence that the preaching of the gospel had ever reached the ' parts lately discovered by the Spaniards, and the antipodes,' how could they come under the comfortable promise : ' Whosoever shall call upon the name of the Lord shall be saved ' ? [4]

Scripture, however, did not merely create the problem by its variance with humane thought ; it crystallised it in its own contradictions. In face of the texts just quoted how was the ' voluntas salvifica ' of God, expressed in the words ' God will have all men to be saved,' [5] to be understood ? God could scarcely have willed man's salvation, without at least putting within his grasp the revelation of the articles of faith necessary to salvation : without, that is,

[1] So, e.g., Tert., de bapt., 12 ; Origen, in Lev. hom., viii. 3 ; Cyprian, Ep. lxiv. 5 ; Cyrill. Hier., Cat., iii. 10 ; Ambrose, de Abrah., ii. 11 (79) ; Aug., Ep. clxvi. 7 (21) ; de pecc. mer., i. 24 (34) ; de an., i. 9 (11), iii. 9 (12), etc.

[2] Mark xvi. 16 : ὁ δε ἀπιστήσας κατακριθήσεται; Vulg. : ' qui vero non crediderit, damnabitur.'

[3] Soto, de nat. et grat., ii. 12 ; Vega, de justificatione, vi. 18.

[4] Rom. x. 13.

[5] 1 Tim. ii. 4. For attempts to explain the text away (e.g. Estius, Sylvius) see S. Harent, art. ' Infidèles ' in Vacant et Mangenot, Dictionnaire de la Théologie Catholique, vii., 1831–1833.

making accessible to him the preaching of the gospel. If, then, the gospel has not been preached to all nations, it must surely follow that God has not put salvation within the power of everyone, and consequently, that He does *not* wish all men to be saved.

Nor was the difficulty merely that of reconciling texts of Scripture, either with one another, or with the humaner tendencies of the Renascence. Had the scriptural demand for faith been the only ground for proclaiming its necessity, there was an easy way out. Such a demand need bind only ' ex necessitate praecepti '—as a command laid upon man by God ; and since God does not demand the impossible of anyone, where the means necessary to the creation of faith were not to be had, He would most certainly accept a good will in place of the act of faith. But there was a deep conviction in the Catholic mind that faith was necessary, not merely ' ex necessitate praecepti,' but also ' ex necessitate medii ' [1] : that it was by the very facts of the case a *sine quâ non* of salvation. The necessity, in short, was not merely theological, but psychological as well. How could a soul be in a state of grace—on the road to salvation—drawing near to the vision of God—unless it were dominated by the conviction that God was the author, governor, and redeemer of its being ? Faith is essentially a virtue whose object is God ; and without a consciousness of that object there can neither be faith, nor *anything that can conceivably take its place* as a stimulus to, and a stage in, the quest for God. To the validity of this conception of faith as a *sine quâ non* of salvation we must return in the next chapter ; all that is necessary at this point is to note how much it enhanced a difficulty already present. Speculations which would other-

---

[1] On this distinction cp. Suarez, *de fid. theol.*, xii., introd. ; and note Aquinas, *S.T.*, ii. 2, q. 10, a. 1 : The heathen who are entirely ignorant of the gospel ' damnantur quidem propter alia peccata, *quae sine fide remitti non possunt* ; non autem damnantur propter infidelitatis peccatum.' Cp. *ad Rom.*, x., lect. 3.

wise appear nothing more than the misplaced ingenuity of
theological sophistry become intelligible, when it is realised
that one and all were devised to deal with the situation
created by this conviction.

Many theologians found no way out of the labyrinth.
Just as some, following Augustine, would not admit that
any ignorance of the faith could be inculpable in itself,[1] so
others fell back on the unhappy conclusion that this absence
of faith must carry with it ultimate and certain damnation.
Vega [2] gives a list of mediæval rigorists : Hadrian could
only admit invincible ignorance as an excuse in the case of
those who had already ' turned to God ' ; Gerson [3] went so
far beyond the common teaching (that there could be no
invincible ignorance of the law of nature) as to assert the
same of the ' truths of faith,' with the corollary that absence
of faith must always mean formal or pertinacious infidelity ;
William of Paris agreed with Gerson.   The spirit lived on
sporadically even after the Reformation, as was said above ;
neither Roman, Anglican, nor Protestant circles were immune
from it.[4]   Rome undoubtedly set her face against extreme
rigorism.   Among the propositions of Michael Baius of
Louvain, condemned in 1567 and later, were the following :
(No. 25) ' omnia opera infidelium sunt peccata, et philo-
sophorum virtutes sunt vitia ' ; (No. 35) ' omne quod agit
peccator vel servus peccati, peccatum est ' ; (No. 68)
' infidelitas pure negativa in his, (in) quibus Christus non
est praedicatus, peccatum est.' [5]   Jansen and Quesnel continued this ultra-Augustinian tradition ; in 1690 among the

---

[1] *Supra*, p. 5.          [2] *de justif.*, vi. 18.
[3] *de vit. spir. an.*, lect. 3.
[4] See, e.g., Hastings's *Encyclopedia of Religion and Ethics*, art. ' Universalism.'
[5] Denz.-Bann., nos. 1025, 1035, 1068 ; cp. nos. 1040, 1046, 1047.
There is some doubt as to the degree of condemnation involved, owing to
the ambiguity as to the place of a comma in the conclusion of the Bull.
See Loofs, *Dogmengeschichte* [4], p. 679 n. ; and authorities cited in Mirbt,
*Quellen* [3], p. 269.

propositions condemned by Alexander VIII were these :
(No. 2) ' tametsi detur ignorantia invincibilis juris naturae,
haec in statu naturae operantem ex ipsa non excusat a peccato formali' ; (No. 5) ' pagani, Judaei, haeretici aliique hujus
generis nullum omnino accipiunt a Jesu Christo influxum ' ;
(No. 8) ' necesse est, infidelem in omni opere peccare.' [1]

The good sense of Christendom rejected extremes such
as this : but the difficulty of finding a loophole for the
virtuous heathen was severe.  So long as pagans were
thought of as few in number, it was possible to hold that
God would either send to each of them separately a preacher,
or else would illuminate him by a special act of grace.  So,
in the famous passage about the man ' brought up among
woods and brute animals,' [2] St. Thomas says : ' It belongs
to the divine providence to provide for everyone whatever
is necessary to his salvation, so long as he does not oppose
any obstacle.  If therefore anyone so brought up should
follow the lead of natural reason by seeking the good and
avoiding the evil, it is most surely to be held that God will
either reveal to him by internal inspiration what is necessary
to be believed, or will send some preacher of the faith to
him, as He sent Peter to Cornelius.'

Later writers found in this confident assertion the
difficulty that it would involve an unprecedented number
of separate miracles to enlighten all the heathen.  To
the Middle Ages it presented quite a different problem,
which must be noticed for its bearing upon a subsequent
theory.  This imaginary heathen, being unbaptised, is
obviously still in original sin ; as he is living up to the
best that he knows, he cannot be in mortal sin ; but as
no human being capable of moral action can exist without venial sin, he probably has venial sins on his con-

---

[1] Denz.-Bann., nos. 1292, 1295, 1298.  For Quesnel's rigorism cp. *ib.*,
nos. 1379, 1388, 1391, 1398, etc.

[2] *de verit.*, xiv. 11, ad 1.

science. *Now if he should suddenly die, where would he go to ?*
Heaven and purgatory are closed to him ; they are for
baptised believers only. Hell is scarcely the place for anyone not guilty of mortal sin. The 'limbo of the Fathers'
was reserved for the Old Testament saints, who remained
there for a while until Christ illuminated them by His
descent into Hades.[1] The only other destination left is
the limbo of unbaptised infants, where indeed original sin
is ' punished,' ' though with the mildest of all punishments.' [2]
But it is ' inconvenient ' that an adult heathen should go to
the limbo of babes, especially as he has *actual* sin on his
conscience, whilst limbo is reserved for *original* alone.

It is obvious, therefore, that no one must be allowed to
die while in a state of original and venial sin alone. God
must avert such a catastrophe by illuminating the virtuous
heathen (either by inspiration or by messenger) at the very
first moment of his moral life, so that he may at once have
faith and qualify for heaven.[3] And yet the heathen must be
already virtuous to deserve illumination, and this would seem
to imply that, though still unbaptised and unilluminated,
he has received regenerating grace. St. Thomas meets this
difficulty in a series of passages dealing with the ' lad
coming to the use of reason.' [4] He imagines a complicated

[1] *S.T. Suppl.* q. 69, aa. 4–6 ; iii. q. 52, aa. 2, 5.

[2] Aug., *de pecc. mer.*, i. 16 (21) ; *Enchir.*, 93 ; *c. Julian.*, v. 11 (44).
Cp. also on ' limbo,' *de an.*, i. 9, iv. 11 ; *Epp.* 166, 217 ; *c. Julian.*, vi. 4 (10) ;
*de corr. et grat.*, 7 (12). For the rigorist view which consigns unbaptised
infants to hell, Fulgent., *de fide ad Petrum*, 27 (68) ; Greg., *Mor.*, ix. 21 (32).

[3] Being now enlightened, he can obtain ' remission ' of his original
sin by the will to be baptised, even if actual baptism is unattainable.
The unenlightened heathen, on the other hand, is incapable even of the
will to be baptised, since he can never have heard of baptism, and so
must remain in his original sin.

[4] ' De puero perveniente ad usum rationis ' (*S.T.*, i. 2, q. 89, a. 6 ;
*de ver.*, xxiv, a. 12, ad 2 ; xxviii, a. 3, ad 4 ; *de mal.*, v, a. 2, ad 8 ; vii,
a. 10, ad 8 ; 2 *Sent.*, d. 28, q. 1, a. 4, ad 4 ; d. 42, q. 1, a. 5, ad 7 ; 4 *Sent.*,
d. 45, q. 1, a. 3, ad 6). In the third and fourth of these passages St. Thomas
dissociates himself slightly from the view that no one can be in a state of
original and venial sin only.

transaction by which the ' lad,' the moment he arrives at maturity, is faced by a choice between a good and an evil career. If he elects for good, he will at once be illuminated ; if he elects for evil, he is guilty of mortal sin ; in either case the question of his eternal destiny is automatically settled. This solution (about which St. Thomas himself had hesitations) raised more difficulties than it settled. It is not borne out in fact, for only too often ' lads ' reach the age of reason without making, or even contemplating, any such choice. Nor is it satisfactory in strict theory ; a miracle of grace is needed to enable one in original sin to make the virtuous choice, no less than a miracle of illumination to endow him with faith after the choice has been made—the difficulty has only been pushed a stage further back. It is scarcely surprising, therefore, that the ' puer perveniens ' and his spiritual Aeneid became the King Charles's head of succeeding theologians for at least four centuries.[1]

We need not concern ourselves with the ' lad ' any further. St. Thomas's solution, whatever its details and interpretation, depended upon the theory of the special and miraculous enlightenment of individual heathen ; and the discovery of America put any such theory beyond the bounds of reasonable possibility. With the recognition that there were myriads of heathen to whom the gospel

---

[1] The various difficulties and explanations involved are fully given by S. Harent, op. cit., 1863–1894. Fr. Harent himself condones St. Thomas's theory only at the expense of a theological massacre of the innocents : there must be the choice, and the consequent illumination (if the choice is rightly made), whenever ' aux circonstances générales de l'éveil moral vient s'ajouter cette autre circonstance très particulière, que la mort soit tout prochaine, elle aussi.' In all other cases he prefers to think of the gospel coming to the ' puer ' by more natural means.—One of the wisest discussions is that of Victoria (de eo ad quod tenetur homo etc. in the Relect. Theol.). It is distinguished by the fact that to him the ' age of reason ' only begins when moral deliberation begins ; whereas other writers have to wrestle with the difficulty that moral deliberation, though it ought to begin on arrival at the age of reason, commonly does not (op. cit., i, § 27).

had not and could not penetrate, came the necessity of finding some other means of vindicating belief in their ultimate salvation—or at all events the salvation of those of them who lived up to the best they knew. They could not *all* be specially illuminated ; miracles on so colossal a scale are foreign to God's recognised methods of working. ' It is not likely that God would demand as <necessary> means for justification something which could not be obtained without a miracle.'[1] Nor was the supply of preachers sufficient to warrant that the gospel could be brought to every ear. How then are the virtuous heathen to be saved, if they are to be saved at all ?

## II

That Christian thought interested itself deeply in this problem is evidenced by the variety and ingenuity of the solutions suggested. The most popular was one in which the new humanism combined with tendencies which had shown themselves from time to time in pre-Reformation thought. It was held that Christian faith was not universally necessary for justification, but that, where it could not be had, a conscientious acceptance of, or obedience to, the dictates of natural reason would take its place. A late writer, Ripalda, gave to this ' adhesion to the best that a man knew ' the title of ' fides late dicta,' as opposed to the ' strict faith ' in the specifically Christian revelation.[2] Another form of the theory held that the will to believe (' fides in voto ') was enough where the light of revelation had not shone ; just as the ' will to be baptised ' compensated for the lack of baptism where the latter could not be

---

[1] Suarez, *de fid. theol.*, xii. 2, n. 3 ; cp. *de praedest.*, iv. 3. 16 ; *de vit. et pac.*, ii. 8, nn. 1, 2.
[2] Ripalda, *de ente supernat.*, disp. 63, sect. 1.

had.[1] This, however, was not widely held, because (as has already been said) the Church was convinced that faith was essential ' necessitate medii ' as well as ' necessitate praecepti,' whereas baptism fell under the second necessity alone. And further, the will to be baptised implies a knowledge of what baptism is and what it effects ; but it is clear that ' fides in voto ' cannot imply a knowledge of what the faith is, for it is adopted as a theological expedient only in cases where knowledge of the faith is entirely lacking. The proposition therefore that ' fides in voto,' where faith cannot be had, is an effective substitute, just as baptism ' in voto ' is a similar substitute where actual baptism is out of the question, falls to the ground ; there is no analogy between the one emergency and the other.

The doctrine that those, to whom no opportunity of explicit knowledge of the faith had come, might yet be saved by loyally living up to the best they knew, was one of creditable antiquity. Origen had held it, though perhaps more out of logical consistency—it sprang directly from his two great principles of ' the end shall be like the beginning '[2] and ' God shall be all in all '[3]—than from humanitarian motives. But he quoted Scripture for his belief—even Sodom was to be restored, Ezekiel had prophesied ;[4] and from Romans ii. 10, ' it would seem that the Gentiles, though they appear to be severed from eternal life as not knowing Christ, and so unable to enter the Kingdom of God

---

[1] See Suarez, *op. cit.*, xii. 2.   On baptism *in voto* see Ambrose, *de ob. Val.*, 51 ; Aug., *de bapt.*, iv. 21, 22 (28, 29) ; *Conc. Trid.*, sess. vi., *decret. de justif.*, c. 4 (Denz.-Bann., no. 796).   Cp. also the similar doctrine of martyrdom as a substitute for baptism, Tert., *de bapt.*, 16 ; Origen, *in Lev. hom.*, ii. 4 ; Cyprian, *Ep.* lxxiii. 22 ; Cyrill. Hier., *Cat.*, iii. 10 ; Aug., *de civ. Dei*, xiii. 7, etc.   Gerson and Caietan extended the doctrine to include the salvation of unbaptised infants by reason of their *parents'* prayers or desires; Vega (*de just.*, v. 16) argues strongly against them, and so liberal an interpretation was never accepted by the Church.

[2] *de princ.*, i. 6, 2.

[3] *Ib.*, iii. 6.

[4] Ezek., xvi. 53, 55.

because not born again of water and of the Spirit, can nevertheless not lose altogether the glory and honour and peace
of good works.' [1]  Where men had failed to hear the gospel
in this life through no fault of their own, the defect might
be made good in the next—'or what are we to say of the
Britons and the Germans who dwell on the coasts of Ocean,
or among the barbarians the Dacians, Sarmatians, and
Scythians, of whom the great majority have never heard the
word of the gospel, but shall hear it in the consummation of
the age ? ' [2]  It was even urged against him that he looked
forward to the salvation of the devil and his angels ; [3] though
he certainly had hesitations on the point, since once at least
he asserted that, in contrast to the Jews, Lucifer would not
be converted even at the end of time.[4]

Origen however mitigated this stark universalism by
allowing degrees of future beatitude—only the pure in
heart should see God, and in the Father's house were many
mansions of varying degree.[5]  Jerome overstated his errors
when he accused him of saying that ' after many ages and
one restitution of all things, it will be the same for Gabriel
as for the devil, for Paul as for Caiaphas, for virgins as for
prostitutes.' [6]  In this admission of degrees of beatitude
are to be seen the first traces of a doctrine which (in spite
of the caveat of the Schoolmen) becomes of importance
centuries later—the hypothesis namely that there will be a
place for the ignorant heathen in the limbo of unbaptised

---

[1] in Rom., ii. 7.  Other scriptural passages employed by Origen in
this sense are indicated by C. Bigg, Christian Platonists of Alexandria,
p. 276 n.

[2] in Matth. comm., series 39.

[3] Epistola ad amicos (ap. Jerome, Apol. c. Ruf., ii. ; Rufinus, Epil.
in Apol. Pamph. Mart. ; Bigg, op. cit., 278) ; cp. Augustine, de civ. Dei,
xxi. 17 ; and the synodal letter of the Council of Alexandria, A.D. 400
(Jerome, Ep. 92).

[4] in Rom., viii. 9 ; and cp. de princ., i. 6, fin.

[5] in lib. Jes. Nav., xxv. 4 ; in Num., xi. 4, 5 ; xxi. 1 ; in Luc., iii. ;
xvii. ; in Lev., xiv. 3 ; in Matt., x. 3.  Cp. Bigg, op. cit., 280.

[6] Jerome, Ep. 84.

children.[1] At the moment it was the more general universalistic outlook of the Alexandrian which attracted attention both from friends and enemies. His position was shared to a greater or less extent by Diodore of Tarsus, Theodore of Mopsuestia, and Gregory of Nyssa; whilst Gregory Nazianzen had an open mind on the matter.[2] Augustine places universalism of the Origenistic kind first among the heterodox opinions upon eschatology with which he deals in book xxi. of the 'City of God,' but expressly notices that it is sentimentalism rather than laxity of morals which gives rise to the heresy.[3]

When Gottschalk revived Augustinianism in its extremest form in the ninth century, Hinckmar of Rheims applied to John Scotus Eriugena to counter the arguments of the predestinarians. Once again orthodoxy received a shock from the reappearance of Platonism in its Origenistic form; and once again the salvation of all men was asserted on the basis of the text 'God shall be all in all.'[4] 'From evil is wont to turn good,' Eriugena wrote,[5] 'but in nowise good from evil . . . The first evil could not be perpetual, but by the necessity of things must reach a certain bound and one day vanish. For if the divine goodness, which ever worketh not only in the good but also in the wicked, is eternal and infinite, it follows that its contrary will not be eternal and infinite. . . . Evil therefore will have its consummation and remain not in any nature, since in all the divine nature will work and be manifest. Our nature then is not fixed in evil ; . . . it is ever moving, and seeks nought

---

[1] Julian of Eclanum held a somewhat similar theory ; Augustine, c. Julian., iv. 3 (26).

[2] So Bigg, op. cit., 343, 344.          [3] de civ. Dei, xxi. 17, 24.

[4] Eriugena, de div. nat., v. 8 ; cp. 27–31, with copious references to Origen. The de divisione belongs to the later stage of Eriugena's writing, after his studies in Greek philosophy had begun. The earlier de praedestinatione (against Gottschalk) is more orthodox (see, e.g., cc. 16, 19).

[5] de div. nat., v. 26, quoted by R. L. Poole, Illustrations of the History of Mediæval Thought and Learning, p. 55.

else but the highest good, from which as from a beginning its motion takes its source, and to which it is hastened as to its end.' It would appear that Eriugena, like Origen, held a doctrine of stages of blessedness,[1] with which a conception of limbo as the place of relative reward for the ignorant but virtuous heathen would not be wholly incompatible ; but it is not clear that he regarded these stages as more than resting-places in a progress which ultimately led to perfection.

Abailard introduced universalism in a new form. Although Bernard reproached him [2] for denying the necessity of faith, and the Council of Soissons [3] condemned him, implicitly at all events, on the same grounds, his own writings do not bear out his opponents' statement. In the 'Introductio ad Theologiam' he insists upon the necessity of faith,[4] and attacks a theologian who said that the heathen could be saved without it.[5] But he developed the theory of Justin and Clement of Alexandria, who saw in selected pagan philosophers sufficient anticipations of the full faith to qualify them as ' Christians before Christ,' [6] by maintaining *as a fact of history*, and with very apposite arguments, that no nation had ever been without faith in the Trinity.[7] On the matter of principle he was

[1] *de div. nat.*, v. 23, 38.　　　　[2] *Epp.* 187, 190.
[3] Duplessis d'Argentré, *Collectio Judiciorum* (Paris, 1728), I. i. 19 ff. ; and see the *Historia Calam.*, 9, 10.　　[4] *Int. ad Theol.*, i. (Cousin, ii. 9).
[5] *Ib.*, ii. (Cousin, ii. 84). Cp. also passages from the *Scito Teipsum*, quoted *supra*, pp. 10, 11.
[6] Cp. Justin, *Apol.* i. 46 ; Clem. Alex., *Strom.* i. 17, 19, etc.
[7] The relevant passages in the *Theologia Christiana* (bks. i. and iv.) are collected in Martène et Durand, *Thesaurus Anecdotorum* (Paris, 1717), v. 1149 ff. It is true that the *Theologia* appears to be a revised version of the book burned at Soissons, and if the latter was the *Tractatus de Unitate et Trinitate* many of the passages in question do not occur in it. But the text of the *Tractatus* is very defective ; and the *Capitula* seem to show that its original form was much nearer to the *Theologia* (see especially c. 5 of bk. i.). At all events it closed with the assertion that ' fidem Trinitatis omnes homines naturaliter habent.' See R. Stölzle, *Abailard's Tractatus de Un. et Trin.* (Freiburg, 1891). In the *Int. ad Theol.*, ii. (Cousin, ii. 78) there is a passage in which the value of proved knowledge is preferred to that of obedient faith.

therefore fundamentally sound. Where he differed from orthodoxy was in asserting, as Vega also asserted at a later stage, the universality of the faith that justifies, though without the safeguards which give Vega's system its peculiar interest, and with far greater assurance than the facts warranted.

It has already been noticed that universalism was a not unnatural reaction against Augustinianism. So in the fourteenth century, when Thomas Bradwardine, followed to some extent by Wycliffe, renewed the extreme form of Augustinian predestinarianism, there appears to have been a revival of Origenist universalism at Oxford. A mandate of Simon Langham, Archbishop of Canterbury, addressed to the Chancellor of the University in November 1368,[1] demands the condemnation, among others, of the following propositions. (No. 1) ' Every pilgrim (' viator '—the technical term for man in this mortal life), adult or child, Saracen or pagan, even though he die in his mother's womb, shall have a clear vision of God before his death ; and whilst the vision remains, shall have free choice between turning to God or turning away from Him. If at this time he chooses to turn to God, he shall be saved ; if not he shall be damned.'[2] (No. 7) ' Saracens, Jews and pagans, even though of adult years and full intelligence (' adultos et discretos '), who never have had, have, or shall have the act or habitude of Christian faith, may yet be saved by the natural law ' (' de communi lege '). (No. 11) ' Anyone can earn eternal life by the use of his natural endowment ' (' ex puris naturalibus '). (Nos. 27 and 28) ' All men, though condemned in hell, are capable of restoration and beatification (' sunt reparabiles et beatificabiles ') . . . All demons are and ever shall be capable of restoration to the path of beatification.'

---

[1] Wilkins, *Concilia*, iii. 75.
[2] This is an obvious reminiscence, in extreme form, of the ' puer perveniens.'

What had however been a merely occasional phenomenon in the Middle Ages developed into an imposing
theory with the Renascence.  The salvation of the virtuous
heathen, despite their lack of faith, was proposed no longer
as an abstract philosophical conclusion from first principles.
It found new roots in the revived admiration for the great
pagans of classical antiquity, as well as in a genuine solicitude
for the spiritual welfare of the newly-discovered heathen
continents.  An instance of the former motive seems to be
found in the case of Marzio Galeotti († 1494), a professor of
the University of Bologna, who created great scandal by
writing a book which ' opened heaven to all men, whether
pagan or Christian.' [1]  Both motives, however, operated
with Ludovic Vives, who in his commentary on Augustine's
' de Civitate ' [2] wrote as follows upon the famous 47th
chapter of the 18th Book :  ' Nature being unpolluted
with vicious opinion might possibly guide one to God as well
as the law of *Moses* ;  for what these got by the law those
might get without it, and come to the same perfection that
the Jewes came, seeking the same end :  nor was their
difference other then if one traveller should cary an Itinery
of his way with him, and the other trust onley his memory.
So may he also now adaies, that liveth in the faithlesse Iles
of the Ocean, and never heard of Christ, attaine the glory
of a Christian by keeping the two abstracts of all the Law and
the Prophets, perfect love of God and his neighbour. . . .
This hath he that seeth the Lord's righteousnesse ;  so great
a blessing is it to be good, although you have not one to
teach you goodnesse. . . . So the nations that have no law but
nature's, are a law to themselves, the light of their living well
is the gift of God comming from his Sonne ; of whom it is said ;
*He is the light that lighteth every one that commeth into the world.*'

<hr />

[1] S. Harent, *op. cit.*, vii. 1737, from Capéran, *Problème du Salut des
Infidèles*, p. 220, where the original authorities are given.

[2] Dedicated from Louvain, to Henry VIII, July 1522.  The translation is that of J. H[ealy], London, 1620.

Protestantism saw a similar phenomenon : Zwingli's humanism in particular met with much suspicion. In his ' de Peccato Originali' occurs a passage headed ' quod temere judicant qui omnes qui non baptizati sunt damnare solent.' In it he speaks of Seneca as ' vir sanctissimus,' and approves of his ' faith ' ; and in a general summary says : ' This text, *He that believeth not shall be condemned*, must in no way be taken absolutely ; but only of those who, having heard the gospel, refuse to believe. Wherefore infants, and those who have not heard the gospel, are not held by this law, but adults <are bound> by that other—namely, whether the law of God is written in their hearts or no.' [1] His last book, the ' Expositio Fidei ad Regem Galliae,' written shortly before his death in 1531, contains a famous and startling passage, in which he promises his royal correspondent, among other joys of heaven, personal intercourse with ' Hercules, Theseus, Socrates, Aristides, Antigonus, Numa, Camillus, the Catos, the Scipios, and all your own ancestors '—a truly catholic collection. ' There has been no good man,' he adds, ' there shall be no holy mind, no faithful soul, from the beginning of the world to its consummation, whom you shall not there see with God.' [2]

### III

It is obvious that liberalism of this character is hardly consistent with any idea of the Christian faith as unique. Andreas Vega, however, a distinguished Franciscan who had

[1] He was not quite clear, however, whether unbaptised children who suffered the further disadvantage of having heathen for their parents would be saved : ' de Christianorum natis certi sumus eos peccato originali non damnari, de aliorum non itidem ; quamvis, ut ingenue fateor, nobis probabilior videtur sententia.' Even Calvin had taught that unbaptised infants would be saved by the intention of their (Christian) parents to have them baptised. (W. Wall, *History of Infant Baptism*, ii. 180.)

[2] The passage is quoted by Bossuet, *Variations des Églises Protestantes*, ii. 19, as the worst of Zwingli's errors. Cp. also Zwingli, *Serm. de prov. Dei anamnema*, 6, ' non est igitur universalis quod qui fidem non habeat damnatur.'

been present at the Council of Trent, made a bold attempt
to harmonise the two conceptions. In chapter XVI of
Book VI of his commentary on the decree ' Of Justification '
of the Council,[1] he exclaims dramatically : ' sed an praeter
fidem fuerint aliqui justificati, aut possint esse, hoc opus, hic
labor est ! ' The Council, he says, 'seem to have taken the
negative view,' but as they did not give the matter much
consideration,[2] it may be discussed. In chapters XVIII and
XIX he states the common opinion that, whilst faith in God
is necessary for justification, explicit faith in Christ is not,
provided that the believer's ignorance on that head is invincible. But this leads us further : ' verum illud magis urget.'
If there be such a thing as invincible ignorance of God, the
same principle must apply to it—a man who in such ignorance lacks the knowledge of God can hardly be thought of
as damned on those grounds alone (c. 20). But will he be
*saved* by his invincible ignorance ? Is invincible ignorance,
that is to say, of the same efficacy as justifying faith ? If
so, it would appear at least that faith is not unique and
absolutely necessary for salvation, and the distinctive
character of Christianity is gone. Vega saw only one
solution, for the theory of innumerable special revelations
did not appeal to him. He denied, as Abailard also had
done, that invincible ignorance of God has ever existed or
ever can exist. ' At all times and everywhere God has spread
the knowledge of His divinity in the world, so that no one
has ever lacked the faith save by his own fault.' It is a
theological commonplace that there can be no such thing as
invincible ignorance of the natural law ; ' but no one can
obey the natural law, or grieve at disobeying it, unless he is
aware of the sole Master and Ruler and Legislator of the
world.' Sufficient faith, therefore, has always been within
every man's grasp.

---

[1] *Tridentini decreti de justificatione expositio*, vi. 16.     [2] c. 21.

Vega thus makes two assertions : the first, that the only content of faith that is *necessary* for salvation is the belief in God as Lawgiver and Ruler ; the second, that this belief is and always has been universally acknowledged by the light of nature [1] (though he allows that revelation is a useful adjunct to convince men of the fact).[2] The first of these contentions, as we shall see, met with general though not universal acceptance ; but the second, unless carefully qualified, would have reduced the doctrine of the necessity of faith to an inept platitude. What purpose is there in saying ' All men must have faith,' if no man can avoid having faith—if it is there by nature ? Vega admits the difficulty. You might indeed in the circumstances explain the texts, ' Without faith it is impossible to please God,' and the like, as ' indicating simply that faith, however and wherever found, is an " infused virtue," ' or as referring to specifically Christian doctrines with the implication that these are necessary normally, or ' necessitate praecepti,' though not in the strict sense universally. But he himself regards these interpretations as ' evasiones immo tergiversationes.' For his own part, he finds the importance of the text in the fact that it points to the *unique attitude* which must be adopted towards the content of faith if we are to be justified. ' The mind must be made captive into obedience to God ; ' but the minds of pagan philosophers, *though they had the necessary knowledge,* ' were *not* so subjected to the law of nature ' (which took the place of God for them). If they had been—i.e. if they had had the faith which justifies—' they would have been willing to believe in the existence of God even if the arguments for that truth proved fallible.' Their attitude was the attitude

[1] ' Paulus non alia asseruit necessaria fuisse credere quam ea quae lumine naturali docuerat manifesta fuisse philosophis Gentilibus' (c. 22).

[2] ' Requisita semper fuit doctrina theologica, ut partim ex illa partim etiam ex lumine naturali intelligerent homines, ac omnino persuaderentur Deum esse ' (c. 21).

of the logician, not of the devotee ; and that makes all the difference.[1]

Of the two factors which are commonly regarded as making up the uniqueness of Christian faith—the uniqueness of its message and the uniqueness of the believer's attitude—Vega surrendered the first, but emphasised the second all the more.  By so doing he brought all the heathen within the sphere of the gospel—they had never been without the necessary knowledge ;—but made their justification depend upon their adoption of the attitude of faith, as distinct from that of knowledge or opinion, towards it.  In his emphasis on the uniqueness of the believer's attitude he was, as will appear, wholly in accord with Christian sentiment ; but this did not make his surrender of the specifically unique element in the content of faith any the more acceptable.  The Church wanted to maintain both—the unique content and the unique attitude—and not even compassion for the heathen would reconcile her to the surrender of either.  The most that she would do was to reduce to a minimum —though by no means to a negligible minimum—the content of that faith which was essential to salvation.

Of Martinez de Ripalda († 1648), who popularised the liberal theory by inventing the term ' fides late dicta,' little need be said.  He set himself to prove the sufficiency for salvation of ' any sort of knowledge of the good.' [2]  His method of argument is no more than the citation of innumerable authorities, whose obvious meaning he wrests to his purpose quite unscrupulously ; and he ignores almost

---

[1] This account of Vega differs materially from that given by Fr. Harent, *op. cit.*, vii. 1759 ff.  Harent is convinced *a priori* that Vega *could not* at once have accepted the decree of the Council and at the same time admitted the possibility of the salvation of the heathen without specifically Christian faith.  He regards c. 20 as a mere confusion of ideas thrown out ' un peu pêle-mêle.'  The Franciscan's argument is no doubt involved ; but the outline given in the text seems fairly to represent his curiously subtle attempt at a compromise.

[2] Ripalda, *de ente supernaturali*, disp. 63, sect. 2 (§ 7).

entirely the difficulties which Vega so clearly discerned. Nor does he retain the ' uniqueness of attitude ' which character- ised even the broadest conception of faith in Vega's theory ; the only contact which his ' fides late dicta ' has with specifically Christian faith is that, in some vague way, it is thought of as being ' supernatural.' Ripalda's fame rests entirely upon the chance which enabled him to give the new point of view its technical name, and so (incidentally) enabled the Church to label it as heretical. Had it not been for this he would probably have remained in an obscurity as complete as that of his unknown disciples who, forty years after his death, were condemned for propagating his opinions.[1]

The Church, as has just been indicated, compromised with this liberal doctrine only so far as to allow the opinion that less than the *whole* Christian faith was sufficient for salvation. The question turned in the main on the doc- trines of the Trinity and the Incarnation. The passage in Hebrews xi. 6 suggested that for salvation it was enough to believe in the existence and remunerative character of God, though it was agreed that—carried to their logical conclusion—these doctrines would be found implicitly to contain the propositions of the Trinity and the Incarnation. Again it was urged that, before the coming of Christ, men had been saved by explicit faith in God alone. But St. Thomas had stated very clearly that explicit belief in the later doctrines was equally necessary now that Christ had come and the gospel been preached ;[2] and his authority was high. Against it could only be quoted the fact that

---

[1] It was probably G. Estrix at whom the condemnation of ' fides late dicta ' was aimed. His liberalism earned for him the title of ' Abailardus redivivus ' (Sommervogel, *Bibliothèque de la Compagnie de Jésus*, iii. 469 ; cf. Harent, *op. cit.*, vii. 1793–1798).

[2] *S.T.*, ii. 2, q. 2, aa. 7, 8 ; though note the slight hesitation in a. 7, ad 3. Cp. 3 *Sent.*, d. 25, q. 2, a. 1, where the necessity of explicit faith in Christ even for the ' puer perveniens ' is stated.

he had used the instance of Cornelius (as indeed it was
commonly used) to prove that baptism ' in voto ' was
sufficient for justification, and had added the rather loose
phrase, ' et alii similes consequuntur gratiam et virtutes
per fidem Christi et desiderium baptismi implicite vel
explicite.' [1] It is therefore remarkable that in this matter
theologians rejected the Angelic Doctor's considered opinion
as too rigorous.

It is important also that they rejected it on grounds
which were genuinely Christian. Suarez's discussion,[2] for
example, is a diffuse one, and many of his arguments
are of little value. He disposes of St. Thomas's main
contention in a respectful manner by suggesting that it
is concerned only with the necessity of explicit faith in
Christ *as a precept* [3] (which can therefore be set aside by God
where the means of fulfilling it are absent) ; and by agreeing
with it as a whole provided that the words ' vel in re vel in
voto ' are added—which really begs the whole question.[4]
By an ingenious though valid manipulation of scriptural
texts he disposes also of a compromise which divided
' salvation ' into two parts—' justification ' and ' glory '
respectively—and found explicit faith in Christ necessary for
the second, though not for the first.[5] But for himself he
holds quite firmly to the opinion that *implicit* faith in the
Incarnation and the Trinity (i.e. *explicit* faith in God alone)
is sufficient for salvation. His main argument on behalf of
the opinion is that the contrary view makes the new law
more rigorous than the old, which demanded faith in God

---

[1] *S.T.*, iii, q. 69, a. 4, ad 2. In ii. 2, q. 10, a. 4, ad 3, he says definitely
that Cornelius ' infidelis non erat ' even before Peter came to him, but
had ' implicit faith '—enough at all events to ' please God,' though whether
enough to ' save ' Cornelius is not stated.

[2] *de fid. theol.*, xii. 4.

[3] ' In lege gratiae,' ' ratione praecepti ' (*ib.*, n. 3).

[4] *Ib.*, n. 18.

[5] nn. 9, 14. Similarly Vega, *op. cit.*, vi. 19. A parallel doctrine was
held by the Pelagians (Aug., *Serm.*, ccxciv. 2 (2)).

alone.  St. Thomas's view, he says, ' non pertinet ad favorem
sed ad rigorem et restrictionem salutis ; ergo non est
asserendum sine fundamento sufficienti ; praesertim quia
lex praeexistens et favorem concedens ' (in this case the Old
Testament dispensation) ' non intelligitur revocata nisi
sufficienter constet.' [1]  As though feeling that his other
arguments are too scholastic he reverts to this statement
continually ; it is one of those instances in which the
genuine tones of the gospel are to be heard where they are
least expected.  Suarez quotes an imposing list of earlier
theologians who agree with him ; [2] it need only be added
that later writers have accepted the position equally fully.[3]

The faith which was *necessary* for salvation was generally
understood, therefore, to mean explicit acceptance of the
existence of God and His remunerative character, and no
more.  So far theologians agreed with the minimising
tendencies of Vega and Ripalda.  Further than this it
was however impossible to go without denying the uniqueness of the Christian faith ; [4] which as we have seen was
held both on theological and psychological grounds.  The
laxer doctrine was therefore definitely condemned by
Innocent XI in the form : ' fides late dicta ex testimonio
creaturarum similive motivo ad justificationem sufficit.' [5]
Two reasons, clearly, operated—the first that natural
knowledge and inference could not give even the bare
minimum of the necessary content of revelation ; the
second that such inference was utterly different psychologically from the theological virtue of faith.  Of the
second reason more must be said in the next chapter.

---

[1] n. 10, cp. nn. 13, 25.
[2] *E.g.*, Soto, Vega, Medina, Corduba, etc.
[3] See, e.g., references in Pesch, *Compend. Theol. Dogm.*, iii. 273 ; and
cf. Billot, *de virt. infus.*, i. 340–342.
[4] As Suarez saw, *de fid. theol.*, xii. 2, nn. 10, 11.
[5] Prop. 23 of March 2, 1679 ; Denz.-Bann., no. 1173.   Cp. *ib.* nos. 1613,
1642 ff., 1715–1719 (Syllabus of Pius IX).

The first might seem difficult to establish, especially for a theology tied to the confident assertions of St. Thomas that natural reason could clearly prove the existence of God.[1] But even St. Thomas did not hold that it could prove so much about God as was necessarily implied in the doctrine that ' He is and is a rewarder of them that seek Him ' ;[2] and later writers develop the thought. Dominic Soto, particularly, who had at one time toyed with the theory of ' fides late dicta,' is emphatic on reconsideration (' re postea oculatius inspecta ') that natural knowledge cannot give the necessary content to the word ' remunerator.' Natural knowledge cannot tell us that the reward held out by God is supernatural—' et hic est veritatis nervus.' ' For true faith it is necessary to believe that God must bless His family with some kind of contemplation of, and association with, Himself. . . . Now this the philosophers never grasped, but thought the mansion of the blessed lay in the Elysian fields, and that their felicity was a kind of repose—something very far from the enjoyment of intercourse with God. . . . And though Aristotle placed the happiness of the contemplative life in contemplation; it was never more than the contemplation of "separate substances "; he never realised that eternal happiness lay in contemplating God.'[3]

We shall be able to judge better of this refusal to allow

---

[1] *Infra*, p. 103.  [2] *Infra*, p. 104.
[3] *in* 4 *Sent. comm.*, d. 1, q. 2, a. 3. Soto (1494–1560) was a distinguished Dominican who was present for a time at the Council of Trent. He advanced a theory not unlike that of ' fides late dicta ' in the first edition (Venice, 1547) of his *de natura et gratia*, but retracted it in the second edition (Paris, 1549) and in the passage above-mentioned. In *de nat. et grat.* ii. 12, after withdrawing his former view, he tends towards the opposite extreme, and suggests that if God does not send an ' angel or preacher ' to the heathen it can only be because they are not ' doing all that in them lies ' to live a virtuous life ; but adds ' super qua re mallem aliorum audire sententiam quam meam praecipitare.' In addition to the reason given above in the text, he felt it impossible to retain his theory ' quia periculosum esset tantum cognitioni naturali arrogare ' (*ib.*).

the heathen the blessing of salvation on the basis of ' natural knowledge ' of God, when we have considered a little more closely the characteristics of that faith which scholastic theology regarded as essential to salvation.  The theory of ' fides late dicta ' is not indeed without its supporters among Roman Catholic theologians to-day,[1] but the condemnation it earned in 1679 naturally turned speculation into other channels.  Eleven years after its condemnation another curious and obscure error was condemned, which embodied the doctrine of ' philosophic sin.'  It appears to have been a piece of Jesuit laxism taught at Dijon by F. Musnier and others in 1686, and at Antwerp by Alexander Maes in 1690, and denounced at Rome by Antoine Arnauld [2] in the Jansenist interest.  But it is not unreasonable to see in it a further attempt to secure the same results as those at which the doctrine of ' fides late dicta ' aimed. The condemned proposition runs as follows : ' *Philosophic or moral sin* is a human act discordant with the rational nature and right reason ; *theological and mortal sin* is the free transgression of the divine law.  Philosophic sin, however grave, in a man who either does not know God or who is not actually thinking of Him, is a grave sin, but is not an offence against God nor a mortal sin which dis-

---

[1] So especially C. Gutberlet [continuation of J. B. Heinrich], *Theologia Dogmatica*, viii. 493 ff. : ' In general faith must be strict faith.  It is necessary " necessitate medii " ; but only the two truths, " God is and is a rewarder," are absolutely necessary.  These must be believed explicitly, but not always in their strict sense (*im eigentlichen Sinne*).  So it is conceivable that a heathen who knows nothing of the motive of faith (*Glaubensmotive*) might come to a true faith through the motive of reason (*Vernunftmotive*).'  Ib., 503 : ' We have devoted so much attention to this subject from a strictly apologetic interest.  It is our purpose to refute the popular impression that the Catholic Church condemns all heathen and infidels to hell.  But although we admit the probability that faith not strictly so-called is sufficient for salvation, it would in practice be perverse to content oneself with such faith.'  Gutberlet's theory has met with much criticism and little acceptance.

[2] Sommervogel, *Bibliothèque de la Compagnie de Jésus*, v. 288, 1470–1473.

solves friendship with God, nor is it worthy of eternal punishment.' [1]

Here obviously is a statement of quite alarming laxity. Victoria [2] had heard of a theory that where there was no knowledge of God there could be no (mortal) sin ; and had rejected it roundly, on the ground that even a man in invincible ignorance of God had clear guidance from conscience as to what was right and what was wrong. St. Thomas, in his difficult ' puer perveniens ' passages, had made it quite clear that an adult heathen must (by divine arrangement) either have received the faith, or else be in a state of mortal as well as original sin. But the doctrine of ' philosophic sin ' denied all this, and asserted that the heathen in ignorance of God, though he might sin gravely, *could* not be in mortal sin. Nor was that all. The theory countenances almost unbelievable laxness of morals among Christians. It implies that the Christian who does not happen to be thinking of God while he is sinning cannot commit mortal sin ; and further, that this is still the case even though he has deliberately and wilfully put God out of his mind. The accommodating spirit of seventeenth-century Jesuitry could scarcely go further, and we cannot wonder at the prompt condemnation of the doctrine ; but its condemnation closed yet another possible avenue of escape for the heathen.

[1] Denz.-Bann., no. 1290 ; Du Plessis d'Argentré, III. ii. 355, 365 : ' peccatum philosophicum seu morale est actus humanus disconveniens naturae rationali et rectae rationi ; theologicum vero et mortale est transgressio libera divinae legis. Philosophicum, quantumvis grave, in illo qui Deum vel ignorat vel de Deo actu non cogitat, est grave peccatum, sed non est offensa Dei neque peccatum mortale dissolvens amicitiam Dei, neque aeterna poena dignum.' A full and valuable account of the controversy is given in K. Werner, *Franz Suarez*, 354–367 ; cf. also H. Reusch, *Index der Verbotenen Bücher*, ii. 531–539.

[2] *Relectio de eo ad quod teneatur homo cum primum venit ad usum rationis* (in the *Relectiones Theologicae*), i. § 27.

## IV

A third solution, which has never been condemned, gives the discussion an interesting turn.  In 1515 the abbot of Wirtzburg, John Tritheim (Trithemius, † 1519), formerly abbot of Spanheim, wrote a book in elucidation of eight questions put to him by the Emperor Maximilian.  The composition attracted some attention ; and a century later Leander of St. Martin, *praeses* of the English Congregation of Benedictines (a distinguished Oxford man whose name was originally John Jones),[1] included it, under the appropriate title of ' Curiositas Regia,' in a collection called ' Otium Theologicum, seu amoenissimae disputationes de Deo etc.' [2]  With the ' Curiositas ' were bound up the ' Speculum Peregrinarum Quaestionum ' [3] of Bartholomew Sibylla, a Dominican of the fifteenth century, and the ' Pentas Aenigmatum Sacrorum ' of Alphonso Tostado, Bishop of Avila.  The three writers were linked together by an interest in the occult ; and the combined volume justly earns its title, and vindicates the publishers' hope that it will serve as ' amoena quaedam ambulatiuncula,' ' ad quam post seria studia animi graves et excelsi paulisper diverterent.'  Tostado's explanation of his five enigmas (' vouchsafed by divine revelation to Mary, Queen of Castille ') are indeed prolix and uninteresting ; but Tritheim has a *flair* for a good story—witness his anecdotes of the swineherd who left his pigs under the care of a cudgel dedicated to St. Blaise, and of his own personal experience [4] of the somnambulist student who ' clung to the roof like a sparrow.'  It must be admitted however that Sibylla

---

[1] [J. François] *Bibliothèque des Écrivains de l'ordre de St. Benoît* (Paris, 1778), s.v. ' Leander ' ; cp. *Dict. Nat. Biog.*, s.v. ' Jones, John.'  He died in 1636.

[2] Douai, 1621.                    [3] First published 1493.

[4] ' Visa loquor, non vaga relatione audita.'  Both tales are given in question 3.

is the real genius of the three. He was a born raconteur, and his ghost stories have a genuinely supernatural ring;[1] whilst his information about demons and necromancy, heaven and hell, is exhaustive and peculiar.

Maximilian's eight questions are not on the whole very startling—three are concerned with witches and wizards, one with the obscurity of Scripture, two with the problem of faith and reason. But one of them, the second, shows even earlier than in the case of Victoria that new interest in the fate of the heathen which resulted from the discovery of America. ' Since only a small part of the world to-day,' Maximilian asks, ' is subject to the Christian faith, can we hold, without injury to the truth, the common opinion that each man who worships the one God can be saved by the religion which he believes to be true and salutary, apart from the Christian faith, and without baptism, and knowing nothing of the religion of Christ ? ' Tritheim, like Sibylla and Tostado, was deeply interested in the ' receptacles,' or eternal destinies of souls ; and he answers with the assurance of an expert. Repeatedly, emphatically, and without qualification, he asserts that there can be no salvation apart from a knowledge of the gospel, and anathematises the impious pretensions to ' tender-hearted-ness ' of theologians who hold the opposite opinion. It is in this connection that he goes out of his way to seal the fate of the Indians : ' The same holds good,' he writes, ' of those who inhabit the islands recently discovered in the

---

[1] Thus the story of the ghost frozen in a block of ice, which began to speak when the ice melted under the bishop's feet, where it had been put *refrigerii causa* (D. 1, c. 3, q. 4) ; that of the bilingual ghost of William of Corvo in the year 1313, which spoke Latin when interrogated by a ' doctor ' (D. 1, c. 4, q. 2) ; Albert the Great's dream of the boy who fell ' de molendino in ripam in nocte ' (D. 1, c. 8, q. 3) ; the Sicilian hermit who saw the ghost of Theodoric hurled ' in ollam Vulcani ibidem ebullientem ' by John the Pope and Symmachus, whom he had murdered (D. 1, c. 3, q. 3). Sibylla's own ghost story (D. 1, c. 3, q. 4) is pointless, but distinctly racy.

Great Sea (of which there is no mention in the ancient cosmographers), who as we are informed have never heard anything whatever of the Christian religion.' So far he is orthodox enough ; but thereafter comes a startling mitigation of the doctrine. 'If any among those who have never heard of Christ live innocently in accordance with the law of nature up till the day of their death, I do not think we have cause to believe or hold that they will be punished with the " poena sensus " (i.e. in hell) ; though they will be deprived for all eternity of the vision of God <and will suffer that> which theologians call the "poena damni " '—i.e. will share the fate of unbaptised infants.

Tritheim was a daring thinker ; he was a friend of Cornelius Agrippa and master of Paracelsus, and his book on steganography [1] nearly procured his condemnation as a magician.  But here he is doing something which the Schoolmen had unanimously declared to be ' inconvenient,' and which St. Thomas's theory of the ' puer perveniens ' had been especially designed to avoid—he is opening the limbo of unbaptised infants to the adult heathen.  It is therefore all the more remarkable that a contemporary, Seyssel, Archbishop of Turin († 1520), adopted the same theory about the virtuous heathen in a book appropriately published at the sign of the ' homo sylvestris ' (who is artistically portrayed in duplicate in the vignette) at Paris in 1520.  The book is nominally a controversial work, ' On the Divine Providence,' against the Waldenses, but suffers a good deal from the homiletic tendencies of the writer.  The problem, ' utrum ignorantia divinae legis excuset a culpa digna damnatione ? ' is put in part II, chapter 2.

Seyssel takes as his text the incident of the Syro-

---

[1] The science of writing in cypher.  But he made wild claims for himself : an unlimited power of thought transference, for example ; and the useful art of teaching the entire Latin language to anyone in two hours.  See the preface to the *Curiositas*.

Phœnician woman ; and argues that if she, with all her disabilities (which he exaggerates in the best pulpit manner), could arrive at faith without direct revelation, there is no reason why the heathen of to-day cannot do the same. He maintains that Judaism at least was world-wide in extent (on the basis of Psalm xix. 4, ' Their sound is gone out into all lands ') ; and that Christianity is nearly if not quite as much so. Even the ' Mahumetica superstitio ' has helped to spread the name of Christ. He is sceptical, therefore, about the inhabitants of the Indies : ' Even if islands or continents can be found to which the name of neither religion (and especially of Christianity) has ever come, surely their inhabitants often travel by land or by sea to other neighbouring lands in which the faith is well known ? I do not believe there is any land or race so unknown or isolated that rumour has not brought to it the name of Christ.' Ignorance of the faith is therefore inexcusable wherever it is found ; the principle of civil law, ' ignorantia juris non excusat,' holds good in the spiritual sphere.[1]

So far he would seem to have condemned the heathen, virtuous and vicious alike, to hell ; but when pressed on the point he relents. Of the virtuous heathen he writes : ' We ought not to believe that they will be worse off than those who die before they are stained by any actual guilt ; as to whom it is agreed that they are not condemned to eternal torture . . . unless you hold that they are implicated in their parents' guilt—a doctrine utterly abhorrent both to the divine law and to natural reason.' So for the best heathen he admits, as in the cases of Abraham, Melchizedek, and Job, the possibility of a direct revelation (' a Deo vocari atque in viam veritatis dirigi ') and therefore of a place in heaven. As for the rest, ' who keep from what is forbidden in the law of nature, with piety towards

---

[1] Seyssel, *de divina providentia*, pt. 2, ch. 2.

God and honest dealing towards men,' ' I should not like to affirm that they will be punished with eternal torments ; although without faith (which alone opens the gate of eternal life) they cannot enter the celestial wedding feast, because they lack the wedding garment.' He relegates them therefore to a place akin to the limbo of those who die without baptism and actual sin, ' though its name and situation are not known to man, nor openly defined by Holy Writ.'

The Archbishop is not without qualms that he is treating the blameless heathen a little shabbily. He asserts that they will be happy in their limbo : ' Wherever it be that these innocent spirits pass their eternal life, they will thank the divine goodness and think themselves happy as compared with the damned ; and will not envy the felicity of the saints, but will accept their lot with equanimity.' Their happiness will consist in the ' perfect knowledge of natural and supernatural things,' though they will of course suffer the ' poena damni,' exclusion from the vision of God. But he cannot conceal from himself the fact that they may resent being put off with a second best ; and he therefore attempts to conciliate them by painting at length the joys of limbo in quite unusual colours, with a wealth of scriptural illustration. He asserts for example that ' out of ten thousand men you would not find one who would not willingly renounce an uncertain hope of heaven in favour of eternal possession of the joys of earth ' ; and that ' the joys of limbo are infinitely supra-mundane.' [1] He cannot promise the innocent heathen ' gratia justificans neque beatificans,' but he assures them that the grace they are

---

[1] All this is based, without acknowledgment, upon what St. Thomas says of unbaptised infants (2 *Sent.*, d. 33, q. 2, a. 3)—that ' they will no more grieve at not seeing God than a man could grieve at not being a bird or an emperor or king '—' rather they will rejoice because in much they participate of the divine goodness and in natural perfections ' and so ' are not altogether separated from God.' Cp. *de mal.*, v. 3. This opinion was common but not universal ; it is attacked by Bellarmine, *de amiss. grat.*, vi. 6.

to receive is ' vivificans, illuminans, conservans, multi-
plicans et adaugens.' He even suggests that they are
not wholly excluded from the vision of God, 'quia Deus
eos a sui cognitione penitus non excludit.' [1] What more
could a reasonable pagan ask ?

This novel theory, by which the virtuous heathen are
saved from hell by admission either to the limbo of unbaptised infants or to some similar ' receptacle,' has enjoyed
considerable though intermittent popularity since its first
introduction ; [2] and has received in recent times the solid
support of Cardinal Billot.[3] The Cardinal however gives
it a new turn by speaking of the ' great mass ' of the heathen
as ' spiritually non-adult.' This might at first sight appear
to be merely a rhetorical expedient to find admission for
them in the limbo of infants, and so to avoid the ' incon-
venience ' of inventing (as Tritheim and Seyssel did) an
additional limbo of which tradition knows nothing. But
it is more than this. The Cardinal definitely regards only
a few heathen, ' the philosophers and sages,' as adults ;
the rest are to all intents and purposes ' infants.' [4] No
distinction is therefore drawn between the virtuous heathen
and the vicious ; all alike are certain of the relative beatitude of limbo. If this were really so, we must conclude
that it would be better to be a sinful pagan than a sinful
Christian. This anomaly is a fatal objection to the
Cardinal's position ; and if we are to consider the possibility of a limbo for the heathen at all, it is better to take
the theory as it stands in Tritheim and Seyssel. In its
favour is the fact that it avoids the monstrous injustice of
condemning all heathen to the pains of hell because of the
absence of a ' faith ' to which it was impossible for them

[1] They will see God from ' afar off,' not hard by, as the Saints do (*ib.*).
[2] For the writers who have held it see Fr. Harent's article, *op. cit.*,
vii., 1897, 1898. Dante also had previously approximated to it, *Inferno*,
iv. ; *Purgatorio*, vii.
[3] ' La Providence de Dieu ' in *Études*.  [4] *Ib.*, May 5, 1921, p. 272.

to attain ; and does so without descending to the theory of ' fides late dicta,' or postulating immediate revelations on a colossal and unprecedented scale. Against it may be urged the facts that it condemns the heathen, however virtuous, to final exclusion from the vision of God ; and that it violates tradition at one or other of two points— either by introducing into theology a new and utterly unheard-of limbo ; or by crowding adults and infants alike into the limbo of the unbaptised, a thing which the Schoolmen regarded as ' inconvenient.'

So strongly are these objections felt by Fr. Harent, the latest critic of the theory, that he finds himself compelled to reject it. He has however nothing to put in its place except the old hypothesis of innumerable special revelations. The fact is indeed disguised by his enumeration of a long list of ' suppléances providentielles de la prédication,' designed to reduce to a minimum the number of cases in which direct revelation will be necessary. Among these ' suppléances ' he includes miracles wrought in support of preaching ; [1] the influence of laymen, schismatics, Jews, Mahometans, heretics, and even the Bible Societies (of whose condemnation,[2] however, he emphatically approves) ; and finally the survival, in various races, of a primitive revelation of indeterminate extent.[3] It is not to be supposed that Tritheim, Seyssel, or Cardinal Billot would ignore these ' suppléances providentielles ' ; the question at issue is another one. What is to happen where the ' suppléances,' alike with Catholic preaching, have never been known ? Fr. Harent makes up the deficiency with special revelations, the earlier writers with the theory

---

[1] He instances miracles from the life of St. Columba.

[2] See Denz.-Bann., 1718a, and references there given.

[3] He quotes a considerable number of nineteenth-century writers who hold this view (op. cit., 1918–1926). If this point were pressed, it would bring Fr. Harent into line with Vega, with the corollary of involving him in the denial of the uniqueness of the content of faith.

of limbo for those who have ' done what they can ' ; the choice (on the basis of that conviction which regards Christian faith as essential to salvation) seems to lie between the two.

It seems reasonable to suggest that the second alternative—that of a limbo for the virtuous heathen—is the more satisfactory : for the hypothesis of special revelations where everything else has failed is always a dangerous one to adopt. And indeed, if it were recognised that such a destiny could carry with it all the joys so fluently pictured by Seyssel, only one thing stands against the theory— that it still excludes the virtuous heathen from the high joy of heaven itself. But the doctrine of the Last Things has always been so vague and fluctuating even in the West (and still more in the East [1]) that it would not seem impossible for Catholic theology to reconcile itself to one step more—the step namely which sees in this so-called ' limbo ' a preparatory training for heaven itself. Thus it could be brought into line with what has been written by not the least of the historical theologians of our time : ' Few among us would desire to bar the gates of heaven against the Unitarian Channing, against the Buddhist ascetic, against even the naked savage who on his sea-swept coral reef, forsaken as he may seem of God and man, is yet just and grateful and kind to wife and child. Yet few would think that for these maimed souls no instruction is needed, that the mere rending of the veil can make tolerable the splendour which it reveals. We believe in the many stripes and the few. We believe that star differeth from star in glory, and in these words lies all that any sober-minded man has ever maintained.' [2]

---

[1] See the important references and authorities given in C. Bigg, *Christian Platonists of Alexandria*, pp. 345–349 ; especially the instances of unbaptised heathen believed to have been saved by the prayers of Christians.

[2] *Ib.*, p. 350.

However these things may be, our immediate purpose is fulfilled if we notice that in postulating at least a degree of eternal beatitude for the virtuous heathen who receive the gospel from no human lips (and this statement will cover both the theory of Tritheim and Seyssel and that of Fr. Harent) theology simply advanced the doctrine of invincible ignorance a stage further. We have noticed so far three stages in the doctrine. The first was that in which sheer ignorance of a relevant fact or principle was seen (under certain conditions) to free the Christian from the blame of an apparently sinful act committed under the direct influence of that ignorance. The second was that by which the heathen who had never heard the gospel was similarly acquitted of the sin of infidelity. In the third stage a like acquittal was extended to the heathen or heretic who, having heard the gospel, was unable in all good faith conscientiously to accept it. The present chapter has witnessed the admission of a further point : that invincible ignorance of the gospel, though naturally enough incompatible with Christian faith, will not involve the heathen in the fate of eternal damnation. This, it is true, is a position which we have not found explicitly stated in respect of heathen and heretics who, having heard the gospel, are invincibly unable to accept it ; but on the principles already established it may be regarded as an acceptable conclusion, and the affirmations of Pius IX already quoted appear to endorse it fully. One problem still remains to be faced. Those who have principally been considered so far have been, in a wide sense, ' outside ' the Church. On the strict canons of moral theology, how does it stand with those ' within ' the Church ? May they, either in general, or at least on particular occasions, conscientiously disobey the precepts or doubt the tenets presented to them by the Church, and yet remain blameless and capable of salvation ? And, if so, can they in either case claim to retain their membership of the Church, in spite of this deliberate nonconformity ?

To these questions therefore we must turn ; but as a preliminary we must examine a little more closely the scholastic conception of faith.  Such an examination is necessary, also, to enable us to estimate the validity of the two principles with which the present chapter has mainly been concerned :  the principle namely that the irreducible minimum of Christian faith—a minimum, even so, to which the natural reason of man cannot attain unaided— is the conviction of the existence and remunerative character of the one God ; and the principle that without this minimum of faith salvation is impossible.  If these two principles are found to be invalid, we must pronounce the labours of Origen, Vega, Tritheim, and the rest to have been entirely otiose and misdirected.  In seeking to find a way of salvation for the unevangelised heathen, they were battering at an open door ;  they were treating as axioms of the gospel what were no more than the pedantic formulas of a perverted ecclesiasticism.  Theology must decide whether it will stand by principles accepted as undisputed both by the champions of the heathen and by their opponents, or whether a truer reading of the gospel message enables it safely to disown them.

H

# CHAPTER IV

## FAITH AND DOUBT

### I

WHAT, then, is the faith without which a man cannot be saved? It is, in scholastic thought, a specific attitude towards a specific object. The *object*,[1] as we have seen, is at the very least the one God in His capacity as 'remunerator.' Whatever further conviction about God is desirable for salvation, so much is essential. In other words, the attitude distinctive of Christian faith cannot be adopted towards an Olympian pantheon, nor towards a mere First Cause. Neither polytheism nor monism can generate it; it is definitely monotheistic and transcendentalist. We may hesitate for a moment to accept this as a dogma; indeed our acceptance depends on what we learn as to the attitude of faith itself. And for that we must go to school with St. Thomas once more.

Faith, St. Thomas says, is ' the assent of the mind to that which is believed.'[2] Assent—that is to say, ' firm assent without a shadow of doubt,'[3]—is of two kinds. It may either be ' compelled ' by the self-evidence of that to which it is given, as we assent to a self-evident fact or a syllogistic conclusion; or it may be the ' voluntary ' result

---

[1] More strictly the ' material object.'

[2] *S.T.*, ii. 2, q. 1, a. 4: ' importat assensum intellectus ad id quod creditur '; cp. q. 2, a. 1: ' cum assentione cogitare,' where *cogitare* is explained as ' consideratio intellectus cum quâdam inquisitione, antequam perveniatur ad perfectionem intellectus per certitudinem visionis.'

[3] *Ib.*; and ii. 2, q. 4, a. 8.

of an act of will. The former kind of assent Aquinas calls
'knowledge,' 'intellect' or 'vision' (as we say that we *see*
a thing to be true) ; the latter kind is reserved to the act
of faith.[1] This leads him to a number of distinctions not
without importance to his purpose. Thus he points out [2]
that in so far as the assent of faith is 'voluntary' and not
'compelled,' it is similar to 'opinion' ; though (on the
other hand) as opinion is always 'cum dubitatione et
formidine,' whilst faith is 'cum certitudine absque tali
formidine,' faith is in respect of this certainty allied rather
to 'knowledge' or 'vision' than to 'opinion.' [3] He is
not indeed prepared to say that it is as certain as 'sight'
'ex parte subjecti,' [4] but he escapes from the awkward
little dilemma thus presented by insisting that, because its
'cause is more certain,' faith is more certain too.

A further problem is offered by the fact that, as Scripture
assures us, 'the devils also believe.' We cannot think that
their belief is voluntary ; it must therefore be compelled by
the evident truth of what is believed. How then can the
original definition of 'faith' as voluntary be maintained ?
A lesser theologian, daunted by this argument, might have
said that the devils were credited with faith in a metaphorical sense only. But St. Thomas is of sterner mould.
He asserts that the devils do not 'see' or 'know' the truth
of the Christian revelation (and therefore their faith is still
a voluntary assent) ; yet they *do* see (or are convinced), *ex
perspicacitate naturalis intellectus*, that they are forced by 'the
evidence of signs' to make this voluntary act of adhesion.
We are thus left in some perplexity as to the demonic
psychology : and it is no surprise to learn thereafter that
'hoc ipsum demonibus displicet quod signa fidei sunt tam

[1] i. 2, q. 67, a. 3 ; ii. 2, q. 1, a. 4 ; cp. aa. 5, 9 : 'credere' is 'demonstrative non noscere' (q. 5, a. 2).
[2] ii. 2, q. 1, a. 4 ; cp. i. 2, q. 17, a. 6.
[3] ii. 2, q. 2, a. 1 ; q. 4, a. 1, in corp. ; *de verit.*, xiv. 1.
[4] q. 4, a. 8.

evidentia ut per ea credere compellantur ; et ideo in nullo malitia eorum minuitur per hoc quod credunt.'[1]

The demons, however, have brought us to a critical question. Why *does* the Christian believe what he believes, or why *ought* he to believe the teaching of the Church ? Faith is a voluntary assent, no doubt, but there must be some reason for it. A mere light-hearted and unmotived embrace of the Christian truth is obviously not virtuous ; indeed, as St. Thomas's pertinent objector puts it, ' periculose assentit homo in illis in quibus non potest judicare utrum illud quod ei proponitur sit verum vel falsum.'[2] To believe without any reason at all for believing is mere ' levitas '; to believe on insufficient grounds is scarcely better.[3] Yet the one obvious ground for assent has been cut away. We may not believe because the thing is demonstrated to be true —that would confuse faith with ' knowledge ' or ' sight '; and such a confusion St. Thomas will not contemplate.[4] It is at this point that his system diverges most from the lines familiar in modern thought, and we must move carefully. He begins [5] by distinguishing in every intellectual act two kinds of ' object,' ' id quod materialiter cognoscitur ' and

[1] ii. 2, q. 5, a. 2. The explanation in *de verit.*, xiv. 9, ad 4, is similar, though here he admits that ' fides aequivoce dicitur ' in the two cases. The distinction seems to envisage three propositions : (1) ' I see this to be true'; (2) ' I see this to be worthy of credence (' credibile ')'; (3) ' Though I do not see this to be true, I see that I must believe it (' credendum ').' The first is the attitude not of faith at all, but of knowledge ; the second of human faith ; the third of demonic faith. St. Thomas assumes (but does not prove) that there is a nice yet genuine distinction between (3) and (1).

[2] ii. 2, q. 2, a. 3, obj. 2.

[3] a. 9, obj. 3; cp. Tert., *adv. Marc.*, v. 1 ; Justin, *Apol.*, i. 53 ; Aug., *de praed. sanct.*, ii. 5.

[4] Because (1) you cannot *know* and *believe* a thing at the same time (i. 2, q. 67, a. 3, in corp., and ad 1 ; ii. 2, q. 1, aa. 4, 5, etc.—here later theologians differed from him, and he himself was not quite clear on the point —cp. ii. 2, q. 2, a. 10 : Suarez, *de fid. theol.*, iii. 9, n. 5, and authorities there quoted) ; (2) the objects of faith, whilst never contrary to human reason, are beyond the compass of its understanding (ii. 2, q. 1, a. 4 ; q. 2, a. 3 etc.) ; (3) to believe on compulsion is not ' meritorious ' (*infra*, p. 111).

[5] ii. 2, q. 1, a. 1.

'id per quod cognoscitur.' These correspond to the 'What?'
and the 'Why?' of belief respectively ; and so (as he recognises) though we may rightly call the former the ' material
object,' it is safer to speak of the latter not as the ' formal
object ' but as the ' formalis ratio objecti.' Thus if a man,
a donkey, and a stone are all seen, they are respectively
' material objects ' of vision, but the ' formalis ratio objecti '
in each case is the same—namely the colour [1] which makes
it a definite object of vision. In the same way, in geometry,
the conclusion of a proposition is the ' material object ' ; the
arguments leading to the conclusion are the ' formal reason.' [2]
How stands it then with faith ? Its ' material object ' is
obviously God and His revelation of Himself as propounded,
for example, in the creeds [3] or the teaching of the Church ; [4]
but what is the ' formalis ratio objecti '—that which induces
us to believe ? We cannot answer ' logical demonstration,'
for it is obviously untrue in fact, and confuses ' faith ' with
' knowledge.' Nor can we answer ' divine grace and that
alone ' ; for though faith is indeed an ' infused ' virtue and
the means of its infusion is grace,[5] if there were nothing else
but grace which caused us to believe, freedom (on this hypothesis no less than on the former) would be violated. What
then are we to say ?

In q. 1, a. 1, of the ' Secunda Secundae ' St. Thomas says
that the ' formal reason ' of faith is ' nihil aliud quam veritas
prima,' and we begin to fear that we are to be launched into
abstract metaphysical conceptions. Luckily, however, he

---

[1] S.T., i, q. 1, a. 3 ; cp. a. 7. Why *colour* and not *light* is explained,
*de verit.*, xiv. 8, ad 4.

[2] ii. 2, q. 1, a. 1. In what follows the word ' motive ' will normally
be used as the English equivalent for ' formalis ratio.' This use would
seem to be justified by the common inclusion of ' God and His revelation '
among the ' motiva credibilitatis.'

[3] ii. 2, q. 1, aa. 8, 9.

[4] q. 5, a. 3. These are at all events implicitly contained in the *minimum*
belief that ' God is and is a revealer ' (q. 6, a. 3).

[5] ii. 2, q. 2, a. 3, ad 2.

spares the reader by adding at once : ' non enim fides de quâ loquimur assentit alicui, nisi quia est a Deo revelatum ; unde ipsi veritati divinae fides innititur tamquam medio.' This is fairly clear ; we believe the Incarnation, St. Thomas says, because we hold God to have revealed it, and because we hold God's revelations to be true. Much the same is said in article 10 of question 2 : ' debet homo credere non propter rationem humanam ' (here for a moment he seems to admit that it is possible for the same man both to *see* and to *believe* one and the same thing) ' sed propter divinam auctoritatem.' [1]

But what do we mean by ' holding ' that God is true and that such and such a thing is revealed by Him ? Is this ' holding' the certainty of ' faith,' or the certainty of ' knowledge,' or the uncertainty of ' opinion ' ? If the first (as Suarez later thought), then faith is built up on prior faith, and so we should have either an infinite regress or a vicious circle. If the third, then faith depends upon the shakiest of foundations—it would be an ' assent with doubt and fear ' —'levitatis est credere.' [2] St. Thomas therefore elects for the second alternative—' per scientiam gignitur fides ' [3]— though not as boldly or as happily as might be wished. Indeed his difficulty is apparent ; if (as he would seem to hold) we *know* that God is true, and that He has revealed such and such a thing, are we not *forced* syllogistically to the conclusion that this thing also is true ? [4] What then has become of the freedom of faithful assent, and consequently (though we are not ready as yet to be dragged into this discussion, which troubles our author not a little) [5] of the merit of faith ? His answer would probably be, that though we

[1] Just as a virtuous act ought to be done not because of a momentary emotion, but because of a virtuous habit (q. 2, a. 10).

[2] q. 2, a. 9, obj. 3.

[3] ' As Augustine said,' q. 6, a. 1, ad 1.

[4] This is de Lugo's position (*infra*, p. 125), mitigated only by the fact that he regards our knowledge of God's truth and revelation as being, not discursive, but immediate or intuitive.

[5] q. 2, a. 9, and *passim*.

*know* God to be true in what has already been revealed, and
know *this* new ' truth' to be revealed by Him, we do not
*know* that He is true in respect of this ' truth.'   There is no
demonstration that can prove it ;  we embrace it therefore
not by a necessary recognition of its truth, but by the free
(yet reasonable) assent of faith.[1]  The reasonableness of
faith is shown both by its being based upon, though not
syllogistically deduced from, prior knowledge ;  and by the
fact that further reasons may be imported to show that
' what is proposed is not impossible.' [2]

On the subject of this prior knowledge St. Thomas is
not without ambiguities.  He asserts that certain things
which ' are proved demonstratively by philosophers ' are
' necessary preliminaries to the things which are of faith,'
and among these ' praeambula ' (as he elsewhere calls them [3])
he includes the existence and unity of God, ' et alia hujusmodi.' [4]  But he does not allow this demonstrative knowledge of the existence and unity of God to carry us far, for
he says :  'multa per fidem tenemus de Deo quae naturali
ratione investigare philosophi non potuerunt, puta circa
providentiam ejus et omnipotentiam, et quod ipse sit
colendus ;  quae omnia continentur sub articulo unitatis
Dei.' [5]  So that we may speak of the very ' existence ' of God

---

[1] This conclusion is ' collected ' (as St. Thomas would say) from the
argument of ii. 2, q. 5, a. 2, where (speaking of the demons) he mentions a
form of faith in which ' intellectus convincitur ad hoc quod judicat esse
credendum his quae dicuntur, licet non convincatur per evidentiam rei.'
It is true that this kind of faith ' non laudatur in fidelibus Christi,' but the
reason is that in them (as distinct from the demons) the ' evidentia
signorum ' does not *convince*, but only proves *credibility* (cp. q. 1, a. 4 ;
*supra* p. 100, n. 1 ; and *infra*, p. 106).    Cp. *de ver.*, xiv. 1 : ' intellectus
credentis tenetur terminis alienis et non propriis.'

[2] *S.T.*, ii. 2, q. 2, a. 10, ad 2 ; cf. q. 1, a. 5.

[3] i, q. 2, a. 2, ad 1 ; ii. 2, q. 2, a. 10, ad 2.

[4] ii. 2, q. 1, a. 5, ad 3, ad 4 ; a. 8, obj. 1 ; cp. *contra Gent.*, i. 3.   In
*contra Gent.*, i. 10, 11, he argues (against Anselm) that the existence of
God is not a self-evident truth ;  in 12 and 13 that it is demonstrable.
The latter proposition is *de fide* in the Roman communion—see *Conc.
Vat.*, Sess. 3, can. 1 *de Rev.* (Denz.-Bann., 1806).

[5] q. 1, a. 8, ad 1.

as being ' believed ' as well as known (and indeed the text
Hebrews xi. 6 forces us to do so[1]), but we retain the distinction between knowledge and faith if we assume that
what the philosophers can *prove* to us is the bare fact of a
First Cause ; whilst the Christian content of that conception
—His providence, His omnipotence, His unique worship-
fulness—is all embraced by faith.[2] ' In the existence of God
<as embraced by faith>,' he says in a fine passage, ' is
included all that we believe to exist eternally in God, that
namely in which our <final> beatitude consists; whilst
faith in His providence includes all that God has ordained
temporarily as means to our salvation, which makes up
the road to beatitude.'[3] Clearly, therefore, those who, at
a later date, denied that natural reason could arrive at even
the necessary minimum of the content of Christian faith,[4]
were following strictly in St. Thomas's footsteps.

Frequently, however, he does not leave to demonstrative knowledge even the bare principle of the First Cause.
Some have not the ' demonstration ' of this, and therefore
must perforce fall back on faith.[5] Lack of ' demonstration '
may be due to an unfinished education—for theology is the
last of the sciences to be taught, and only completes a curri-
culum of many stages; or to dulness of intellect; or to the
cares of life ; or to laziness in learning.[6] St. Thomas even
contemplates a possibility which would wreck his entire
system. Demonstrative proof may be incapable of ever
conveying absolute certainty : ' quia philosophi de rebus

---

[1] *S.T.*, ii. 2, q. 1, a. 7.

[2] a. 8, ad 1. In *de verit.*, xiv. 9, ad 8, this is put more explicitly:—
' unitas divinae essentiae talis qualis ponitur a fidelibus, scilicet cum
omnipotentia et omnium providentia et aliis huiusmodi quae probari
non possunt, articulum <fidei> constituit.'

[3] ii. 2, q. 1, a. 7.

[4] *Supra*, p. 85.

[5] ' Opportet ea saltem per fidem praesupponi ab his qui eorum demon-
strationem non habent ' (ii. 2, q. 1, a. 5, ad 3).

[6] q. 2, a. 4 ; cp. *c. Gent.*, i. 4 ; *de verit.*, xiv. 10.

humanis naturali investigatione perscrutantes in multis erraverunt, et sibi ipsis contraria senserunt.' If this be true ' de rebus humanis,' how much more true ' in rebus divinis.' [1]

The ' preambles of faith,' in the sense of the knowledge out of which it is born, have become sadly reduced in the course of this discussion. For no one can they be more than the bare demonstrative knowledge of the existence of God ' et alia hujusmodi ' ; for many they are not even this. Alongside this, however, St. Thomas puts other known facts about which he is much more certain, though his certainty only leads us further away than ever from modern methods of thought. There is first of all the fact that such and such things have been revealed by God ; this is obvious, for the teaching of the Church and the words of Scripture form an ' infallible rule ' of revelation.[2] Again there is the evidence of signs, ' vel aliquid hujusmodi,' [3] which as we have seen are convincing to the demons, with their perspicuous intelligences, though to men they are no more than ' sufficiens inductivum.' [4] Among these signs are numbered, of course, miracles, prophecies, and preaching ; [5] the invitation of God in the soul ; [6] and we must fairly add, ' the reasons adduced by the saints to show that the articles of faith are not impossible.' [7] The faith of our elders and betters is also contributory evidence, ' for as is said in Job i. 14, *The oxen were ploughing and the asses feeding beside them ;* so the young, who are meant by the " asses," should in matters of belief adhere to their elders, who are signified by the " oxen," as Gregory explains in 2 *Moral.,* c. 17.' [8] All these give

---

[1] *S.T.*, ii. 2, q. 2, a. 4, *in corp.*

[2] ii. 2, q. 5, a. 3 ; cp. *de div. nom.*, i. 1, and especially *de verit.*, xiv. 10, 11, where, speaking of the Old and New Testaments and the Church, he says, ' omnia media per quae fides ad nos venit suspicione carent.'

[3] q. 1, a. 4 ; cp. a. 5, ad 1.

[4] q. 2, a. 9, ad 3.

[5] q. 2, a. 1, ad 1 ; a. 9, ad 3 ; q. 6, a. 1.

[6] q. 2, a. 9, ad 3 ; cp. the fine passage in *cont. Gent.*, i. 6.

[7] q. 1, a. 5, ad 2 ; cp. *cont. Gent.*, i. 9.　　　　[8] q. 2, a. 6.

*knowledge*, the knowledge namely that what is proposed is ' credendum ' or ' credibile ' [1]—i.e. may be believed without imprudence—but they do not compel assent to what is proposed, for they do not *prove* that what is proposed is true. It is on this basis, combined with the logical certainty of the existence of God, that we give the assent of faith to the things which are proposed ; and if we are not certain of the existence of God by demonstration, then, on the same basis of ' evidentia signorum ' and ' rationes inductivae,' it must be assumed that we assent to that existence, as a credible hypothesis, by the same act and in the same way as we assent to the credibility of what is proposed.

## II

Putting these things together, we see that St. Thomas's system is something as follows : (1) The rational man knows that God is, and that He is all-knowing and all true ; or, if he does not know it demonstratively, he infers its credibility from the evidence of signs, as to which he has no doubt. (2) He knows also that something is proposed to him as revealed by God. (3) He has grounds for concluding (' evidentia signa '—which later theologians called ' motives of credibility ' [2]) that this alleged revelation may fairly be accepted as a truth about God revealed by Him, in spite of the fact that reason has not demonstrated it to be true ; he has also grounds which prevent him from concluding that it is wholly unbelievable. (4) He therefore assents to it, by the act of faith, as being revealed by God and true. (5) What moves him is obviously *not* that it is proved to be true, for that is *ex hypothesi* out of the question ; but something

---

[1] q. 1, a. 4 ; but not the conviction that it *must* be believed ; that is reserved to the demons only. ' Credendum ' in this passage appears to be loosely used for ' credibile.'

[2] Commonly, however, ' motives of credibility ' and ' preambles of faith ' are treated as indistinguishable.

else, which St. Thomas calls the 'authority of God as revealer.'

Here is a system at first sight too scholastic and remote to be of any value to the modern mind. Yet it is not justifiable to reject it out of hand. Western Christendom, relying upon it, made those two assertions of fundamental importance which dominated the discussions reviewed in the preceding chapter : (1) that Christian faith is only possible on the basis of a transcendentalist monotheism (God as one, and as a rewarder) ; (2) that without this faith salvation in the full sense of the word is impossible. It is true that these assertions may still hold good even if the scholastic system is found to be untenable. But if it appears on examination to be in principle, if not in all its details, in accord with what Scripture and Christian experience show to be true, we shall have the greatest possible hesitation in rejecting the two assertions which all who have held the system have unanimously agreed to be implicit in it. It has appeared, further, that whereas St. Thomas found the greatest difficulty in admitting the blamelessness of those who after consideration were unable to accept the ' faith,' to his successors, Dominicans and Jesuits alike, this admission presented no difficulty ; and it is only by appreciating the truth and adequacy of his system that we can decide whether he or they were right. We have, finally, to consider the problem of Christian doubt ; and because doubt is the converse of faith, we cannot estimate its culpability or blamelessness without some prior theory of faith. For all these reasons we must ask the question, what relation has St. Thomas's system to the ' faith ' of which Scripture and the experience of Christendom have to tell us ?

We may tabulate the difficulties of his system ; and they are many. The modern mind, unlike St. Thomas, cannot rest secure in the conviction that the existence of God can be demonstrated by reason. Nor can we, as he could, contemplate the mysteries of the Trinity and the Virgin Birth, and say in face of them that it is ' impossible for faith and reason ever to disagree.' [1] The contrast between the ' necessity ' of demonstration and the ' voluntariness ' of faith is strange to us ; and we fail to see how faith can at once be, in any true sense, undetermined by the evidence and yet reasonable. Still less do we accept his unshaken opinion that the words of Scripture and the creeds of the Church are ' above suspicion ' as witnesses to *what* has been revealed by God. But, above all, it is not at first sight clear what he means when he says that the *only* possible motive, or ' formal reason,' for Christian faith is the ' authority of God as revealing.'

It is this last point perhaps which troubles us most, for without it the whole structure is unintelligible. Why this constant emphasis on revelation, and on the authority of God ? No doubt St. Thomas's mode of thought and canons of revelation are very different from our own. But if we grant (for the moment) that the act of faith is something other than the logical conclusion of a train of reasoning, we must find other grounds for vindicating it as a reasonable and moral proceeding. If a man gives a ' firm assent ' to any proposition, he must do it on *some* authority—either that of reason or of someone or something else. He may indeed say, ' I accept the faith of the saints on the authority of the saints, or the faith of the Church on the authority of the Church ' ; but he has still got to say *why* he accepts the authority of the saints and the Church. If he says, as he may well say, ' It is the holiness of life in the saints, or the triumphant progress of the Church,[2] which convinces me that what they say in this matter is true,' he has to meet the argument : ' But neither holiness nor success is a criterion of infallibility ; many holy men have been incurably stupid

---

[1] *de verit.*, xiv. 10, ad 7.
[2] Cp. *Conc. Vat.*, Sess. iii, *Constit. de Eccl.*, 3 (Denz.-Bann., 1794).

and misled ; cynical and un-Christian institutions have been visited by unprecedented success.' In the long run he is forced back to the position, ' I cannot believe that God in a matter of such moment would allow the saints and the Church to err ; they may (if you will) err in other matters, but not in this.'

We are not concerned with the reasonableness of such a statement, but with its implications. Philosophically it takes the form, ' I cannot believe it can be otherwise, the universe being what reason assures me it is ; and therefore I affirm that it is so.' This is indeed analogous to the act of faith, for it is an affirmation of, or an assent to, something not demonstrably proved ;—' I cannot believe it can be otherwise ' is not the same in content as ' I see it to be so.' But the Thomist, as a theologian, includes in the phrase ' the universe being what reason shows it to me to be,' the affirmation (either as a fact, or as a credible hypothesis), ' Reason tells me that God is and is the author of the universe.' To him therefore the act of faith ultimately takes the form, ' I cannot believe it can be otherwise, God being what reason tells me He is ; and therefore I affirm that it is so ' ; or, to bring it nearer to St. Thomas's form of statement, ' God being what He is would not allow the truth to be otherwise, and therefore I affirm it.' This brings us to the conclusion (identical in effect with that of St. Thomas) that the ultimate ground of faith is : (1) God's character as known, or at least postulated on legitimate grounds, by reason and experience ; (2) the congruence of the proposed article of faith with that character.[1]

---

[1] It will be noticed that we have included in the ' objectum formale,' or motive, of faith the ' fact that such and such a thing has been revealed.' This is in accordance with the Thomist tradition ; the Scotists maintaining that such a fact was only a *sine quâ non* of faith. The point is not of importance, and as we have seen (*supra*, p. 103) does not (as with de Lugo) involve the conclusion that the act of faith is discursive. (See Tanquerey, *Synops. Theol. Dogm. Spec.*, i. p. 42 ; Pesch, *Compendium*, iii. p. 240.)

We have indeed substituted for the phrase 'God has revealed it,' the phrase 'God has allowed it to be believed, and it is in accordance with what we know of God.' But the substitution, though marking the difference between St. Thomas's thought and ours, does not affect the essential identity of the two modes of speech. To St. Thomas, 'it is revealed' meant, simply, that the doctrine in question was asserted by Scripture and the Church—witnesses, both of them, above suspicion. To many Christians it still means the same thing ; they hold—not necessarily on insufficient grounds—that the authority of these two witnesses is sufficient to guarantee revelation. But for those to whom such a conclusion remains not proven, the words 'it is revealed' still carry an implication identical in all fundamental particulars. They may prefer to avoid the dangerous term 'revelation'; but the phrase we have proposed—'a statement about God which God has permitted to be known, and which is in accord with all that we already hold to be true about God'—involves neither less nor more than the traditional sentence, 'a thing which God has revealed.' All knowledge of God which is congruous with what is already known about God must, in some way or another, have come from God ; and exactly this is what 'revelation' implies. Indeed, if a Christian who preferred the traditional terms were required to state the criterion by which he differentiated a 'true' from a 'false' revelation, he would be forced in the end to fall back on the test of congruence with the known character of God. Even if he said 'I hold only that to be revealed which is proposed to me by Scripture and the Church,' he would still, if pressed, have to add 'and I hold that what Scripture and the Church propose to me, and that alone, is revealed by God, because the fact that Scripture and the Church should have been chosen as the sole instruments of revelation is in accordance with God's character as a whole as it is known to me.'[1]

Interpreting therefore St. Thomas's ' motive ' of faith— ' the veracity of God and the fact of revelation '—in the sense of ' the character of God as already known or postulated on reasonable grounds, and the congruence of the proposed doctrine with that character,' we see that his statement is not only in itself tenable, but also true to the facts of Christian faith. Indeed, no other form of statement is possible if on the one hand faith is to be not wholly unreasonable, and yet on the other something quite distinct from the act of accepting the conclusion of a logical demonstration. And here we have to face another difficulty. Is St. Thomas's distinction between demonstration as ' necessitating ' assent, and the ' evidentia signorum ' as leaving it voluntary (though pointing to it as reasonable) a fair one ? ' I see it to be so ' is no doubt an assent necessitated by preceding argument and testimony, but is not ' I cannot believe it to be otherwise ' equally necessitated ? Or, alternatively, granted that assent to demonstration and self-evidence is compulsory, whilst faith is not, how can the latter be as ' certain ' as the former ?

### III

St. Thomas insisted on this distinction partly, at least, because without it he could not vindicate the ' merit ' of faith. The term ' merit ' has gained an evil reputation in

[1] This is confirmed by the fact that Roman theologians, with only a few exceptions, admit that a man can reach the conviction that a doctrine is revealed on other grounds than that it is proposed to him by an infallible Church. So Tanquerey, *Synopsis Theol. Dogm. Spec.*, i. p. 47 : ' ad actum fidei divinae non requiritur propositio publica, sed . . . sufficit ut quis per seipsum cognoscat aliquam veritatem esse revelatam.' See Suarez, *op. cit.*, iii. 10, nn. 9, 10. But the infallible proposition by the Church is, of course, a sufficient and, it may be added, the normal ' motivum credibilitatis ' (*Conc. Vat.*, Sess. 3, c. 3, Denz.-Bann., 1794). Cp. Billot, *de virt. inf.*, p. 269.

theology; we shall understand our author better if we interpret it merely as meaning, for our purposes, 'praise-worthiness.' For reasons which will appear it was all-important to him that the praiseworthiness of the Christian's faith should not merely be maintained, but also fully emphasised. We should all agree, it may be supposed, that the ideal Christian faith is reasonable, and that reason, what-ever its limits may be, must in the end move and point Godwards. Indeed we can say that the reasonableness of faith is a *sine quâ non* of its praiseworthiness; for an assent utterly without reason would be a mere act of folly or levity. We should also agree that, though reasonable, it does not carry with it necessity *of the same kind* as a logically demonstrated proposition; we do not so much infer that the Incarnation or the Atonement is true, as believe that it must be true. But the movement of nineteenth-century thought, with its stress upon the non-rational element, the 'illative sense,' in *every* act of judgment, has tended to elevate what St. Thomas would call 'rational proof' into an assent of the same character as the act of faith; it has assimilated the act of reason to the act of faith.[1] This—if we may say so—appears at first sight to have robbed the conception of faith of its characteristic of unique praise-worthiness. It is true that in extreme cases, as of those whose faith in the divine goodness remains unshaken in face even of the bitterest sorrow or the most intense and prolonged suffering, we do regard faith as praiseworthy, and as in the true sense a virtue or 'habitude disposing a man towards God.' But such praise is reserved for cases of this kind; the normal belief of the normal Christian is rarely thought of as being more pleasing to God than any other legitimate assent to a reasonable proposition, because the two forms of assent are now regarded as *in pari materia*.

---

[1] Passages illustrative of this tendency are quoted, *Some Principles of Moral Theology*, pp. 98–101.

But the fact that other forms of assent, which to St. Thomas were, as necessitated, unworthy of praise (though in no way worthy of blame), are now regarded as themselves partaking of the character of an act of faith, is no reason for denying to the latter its meed of praise.   Indeed, when we consider the amazing implications of the series of propositions about God, His character and His love, which go to make up the content of Christian faith ;  the small distance which reason can go in vindicating their truth ; and the grave character of the hindrances and obstacles which have to be overcome ;  it is arguable that the changed attitude towards what is called ' logical proof ' has not conferred upon assent to the latter merit in any way proportionate to that which still remains the glory of faith. We may still hold, with St. Thomas, that faith in any man is not indeed a thing altogether unexpected (for it is still reasonable), but something nevertheless very wonderful, ennobling, and virtuous.   It can never be reduced to the level of the other assents which we still call ' rational ' —assents of a scientific or practical or historical kind— however much the two may be assimilated ;  for the reason that, in experience, men are commonly found to agree to the latter when the evidence and arguments for them have been duly expounded, but only too often do not accept the former.[1]

---

[1] It is to be noticed that Cardinal Newman, who is largely responsible for the tendency to assimilate assents of every kind (e.g. to so-called ' logical ' propositions) to the assent of faith, recognised that, if the Catholic tradition were to be maintained, something must be done to vindicate the unique character of faith.   Obviously enough, he could not use St. Thomas's argument as to the greater ' freedom ' of the assent of faith, having just destroyed its basis ;  nor does he so much as allude to it. But he abandons his customary method of argument from observed facts (' the common voice of mankind '—*Grammar of Assent*, p. 344), and does not base the uniqueness of faith, as he might have done, upon the uniqueness of its results ;  but rather upon dogmatic considerations of an unconvincing and, in the circumstances, an inappropriate character (*op. cit.*, pp. 186, 187).

Nevertheless it would seem wiser to abandon, at all events for the present day, St. Thomas's distinction between assent to reasoned truth as ' necessitated,' and faith as ' free ' ; and to concentrate rather upon his distinction between the former as indifferent and the latter as praiseworthy or ' meritorious.' It is, after all, for the sake of this second distinction that he lays so much stress upon the first. *We* see a large part of the merit of faith in the fact that it believes, on the basis of such and such evidence and arguments, against the weight of apparently contradictory evidence and arguments. St. Thomas could not insist upon this aspect of the case (although he recognised it [1]) because of his conviction that ' reason ' and ' faith ' cannot ultimately disagree.[2] The intensity of that conviction led him partially at all events to ignore the vast number of instances in which as a matter of fact (though perhaps for the time only) reason and faith *do* disagree. His passing comparison between faith and opinion is the one which is to-day all-important, for the essence of faith to us is that it accepts, like opinion, a proposition in the face of some degree of evidence to the contrary ; that it adheres firmly (though in this ' firmness ' it is *unlike* opinion) to one side of the question, for which good reasons can of course be urged, in despite of good reasons which can be urged on the other side. It is *this* characteristic of faith, which meant so little to St. Thomas, which to us makes it praiseworthy, whilst assent to a historical or scientific truth seems almost if not quite indifferent.

We may grant then the unique praiseworthiness of faith, which is that for which St. Thomas was contending ; though our grounds for doing so are different from his. But do not the grounds which lead us to hold it destroy at the same time his contention that faith is certain—' absque ulla formidine ' ? We need not think so. The test of the

---

[1] *Infra*, p. 115, n. 1.     [2] *S.T.*, 1, q. 1, a. 1, etc.

certainty with which a conviction is held is, after all, the
degree in which men will commit their lives and all that
they hold dear to it ; and evidence is not wanting that
this is often enough in fact, and always in ideal, the cul-
minating characteristic of Christian faith—that it produces
heroic and superhuman lives.    And this also is an even deeper
ground for the assertion of the supreme praiseworthiness
of faith—not merely that it believes in face of the difficulties
of belief ; but that it believes, actively and operatively, in
face of all temptations which would force it back into the
category of an ineffective or wayward opinion.[1]

## IV

We have yet to ask why St. Thomas is so insistent on
the praiseworthiness of faith, and consequently (for him) on
its voluntariness, its difference from reason.    It is true no
doubt that effective—or as he would say ' formed ' [2]—faith
is praiseworthy in the highest degree, though this aspect
of it is not commonly brought into prominence at the
present day.    But what is gained by stressing the point ?
Here, for a moment, must be considered what is meant by a
' theological virtue ' ; for it is in this character that he
constantly regards faith.

A virtue, we need scarcely remind ourselves, is ' the
perfection of a potentiality,' [3] or in other words, a ' good
habitude ' [4] by which ' reason is ordered towards God, and
the lower powers disposed <to act> according to the rule
of reason ' ;[5] or by which (more briefly) ' a man is perfected
to act well.' [6]    But ' good action ' on the part of a man

---

[1] This St. Thomas asserts quite definitely, though he does not make
it his principal ground of merit—e.g. ii. 2, q. 2, a. 10, ad 3 : ' ea quae
repugnant fidei, sive in consideratione hominis, sive in exteriori perse-
cutione, in tantum augent meritum fidei, in quantum ostenditur voluntas
magis prompta et firma in fide.'

[2] ii. 2, q. 4, aa. 3, 4.          [3] i. 2, q. 55, a. 1.          [4] Ib., a. 3.
[5] 1, q. 95, a. 3.                    [6] i. 2, q. 58, a. 3.

is action which ' tends towards his end,'—that is to say towards ' beatitude.' [1]  And human beatitude is of a double kind, the one ' proportionate to human nature, at which a man can arrive by the principles of his nature ; the other exceeding human nature ' (or its ' proportion ') ' at which he can arrive only by divine virtue ; i.e. by some kind of participation in the Divine.' [2]  Virtues therefore which aim at or help to the achievement of the first kind of beatitude are called the moral virtues (the cardinal virtues and their adjuncts) ; those which reach out towards the second are the theological virtues.[3]  This second or supernatural end is of course the ' vision of God.' [4]

All this is very Aristotelian.  It seems to place the end of human life solely in human happiness, only adding to the Aristotelian ideal of the ' contemplative life ' the Christian conception of the ' contemplation ' or ' vision ' of God.  But a definitely Christian turn is given to the whole doctrine by the discussion of ' charity '—the ' root,' ' form,' and ' mother ' of all virtues.[5]  Charity in its highest form is identical with the vision of God—for it is simply ' an association of man with God, a familiar conversation with Him.' [6]  Such ' friendship ' is not possible without ' goodwill,' ' according to which we wish the good of our friend.' [7]  Love to God therefore seeks to ' have its goal in Him, not to derive anything from Him ' ; [8] it is a form of ' honouring ' God.[9]  Here St. Thomas has at last reached recognisably Christian ground without shedding his Aristotelian dress.  Charity, and with it all the other virtues of which it is the ' form,' has its value not merely

---

[1] i. 2, q. 62, a. 1 ; cp. qq. 2, 3.

[2] i. 2, q. 62, a. 1.          [3] Ib., a. 2.

[4] i, q. 1, a. 4 ; q. 12, aa. 1, 4 ; i. 2, q. 2, a. 8 ; q. 3, a. 8 ; ii. 2, q. 44, a. 1, etc.

[5] i. 2, q. 62, a. 4.          [6] i. 2, q. 65, a. 5.

[7] ii. 2, q. 23, a. 1.          [8] Ib., a. 6.

[9] q. 25, a. 1.  It need scarcely be added that love to God must include love to one's neighbour (ib.).

in that it paves the way to beatitude, or earns beatitude
as its reward, but also in that it honours and serves God.
Or, even more definitely, beatitude and loving service of
God cannot be distinguished—they are convertible terms.

So when we come to the question of ' merit ' or praiseworthiness, St. Thomas is able to meet an objection which
is fatal to Aristotelianism. ' By virtue,' says the objector,
' a man appears to benefit himself, and perhaps his neighbour, but not God.' [1] The objection, as here stated, is
based on an argument from Scripture as to the divine
self-sufficiency, but it would be no less cogent if it rested
explicitly on the self-centredness of the whole Greek conception of virtue. The conclusion is the same in either
case : ' It would seem that a man can merit nothing from
God for doing that which is to his own advantage alone.'
St. Thomas admits the objector's contention that there is
no direct advantage to God in human virtue ; but rests
the praiseworthiness of virtue on the ' presupposition of a
divine ordinance.' ' God has laid upon man ('ei deputavit ')
the virtue of acting in order that he may receive merit as a
reward.' This safeguards God's own self-sufficiency, but
asserts quite explicitly that virtue and beatitude is something *demanded* of man—his *due* end, as we are told elsewhere [2]—by divine ordinance. And so he replies to the
objector, ' God seeks not from our goodness (' ex bonis
nostris ') anything of use to Himself, but His glory, that
is to say a manifestation of *His* goodness, which also He
seeks from <all> His works. No benefit accrues to Him
from our service of Him (' ex hoc quod eum colimus '), but
only to ourselves ; and so we receive merit from God not
because our actions benefit Him, but in so far as we act to
His glory.' In other words :—our goodness does not benefit
God ; it does benefit ourselves. But what makes it praiseworthy is *not* the fact that we benefit by it, but the fact

[1] i. 2, q. 114, a. 1, obj. 2.          [2] ii. 2, q. 23, a. 2.

that it fulfils the end of our being which God has ordained for us, and which is the worship and service of God.

This is applied in a later discussion [1] to faith. Here, after saying that a man should believe not on human reasons but on divine authority, he shifts his ground. ' There is a second relation in which human reason can stand to the will of the believer. It is *consequent* to the will when a man has a will prompt to believe, loves the truth which he believes, devotes himself to understanding it, and embraces any reasons he can find for believing it— and in this respect human reason [2] does not exclude the praiseworthiness of faith, but is a sign of greater praiseworthiness.' Here then the will to believe is all-important. And though the ' divine authority ' is still the ' motive ' of belief, the ' motive ' of the *will* to believe can be no other than the natural tendency which man has Godward—the tendency to ' caritas ' or ' friendship with God.' [3]

It appears then that St. Thomas has not one but three grounds for asserting the praiseworthiness of faith : (1) that it is ' voluntary ' ; (2) that it is held not only because of evidence, but also in spite of evidence ; (3) that it is born and developed in an atmosphere of desire to honour God. Of these three, however, he depreciated the last, because his Aristotelian bias led him in the main to think of ' virtue ' primarily in relation to the perfection or happiness of the individual, not to the honour and service of God. The second, in the same way, he depreciated, because he was afraid of emphasising the difficulties of faith, and so making it appear no more than a form of ' opinion.'

---

[1] ii. 2, q. 2, a. 10.

[2] I.e., the operations of reason consequent upon, and subsidiary to, the acceptance of the truth by faith.

[3] So ii. 2, q. 4, a. 3 : ' caritas dicitur forma fidei, in quantum per caritatem actus fidei perficitur et formatur ' ; i.e. love to God is ' finis ad quem ordinatur fides.' Cp. q. 23, a. 8 ; and Pesch's definition of faith as ' obsequium intellectuale Deo exhibitum' (*Compend. Theol. Dogm.*, iii. 249).

He was reduced therefore to making the praiseworthiness
of faith depend upon its ' voluntariness.'

But his statement can be enfranchised from limitations
such as these ; and then the praiseworthiness of faith is
seen to rest, not on the doubtful distinction between the
' voluntariness ' of faith and the ' necessity ' of reason, but
partly on its ' firmness ' in face of difficulty, partly on
the desire to serve, honour, and draw near to God, to which
it gives expression.   Of these it is the latter which provides
the higher reason for praising faith, because it concerns
motive rather than result.   What St. Thomas would probably have said, therefore, if he could have freed himself
from the special circumstances of his time and education,
is that faith is essentially an expression of the Christian's
desire to honour and serve the Maker, Redeemer and
Sanctifier of his being.   Because the Christian loves God,
he desires to believe about Him all the good that can be
believed.   He searches for more and yet more ' truths ' to be
embraced by faith ; and though his respect for reason as
a God-given quality makes him apply the test of reason to
whatever may be propounded to him as being ' of faith,'
he adopts this precaution simply because he aims at finding
a creed worthy in all respects of the God of whom it is
asserted.   It is this quality of faith which makes it in the
fullest sense a Christian and ' theological ' virtue ; it is
this quality in it which inspires the great thanksgivings
for faith received, and prayers for faith's increase, which
ring out from the New Testament.   Faith is a part of the
Christian's loving dedication of himself to God ; this is
what makes it praiseworthy.

St. Thomas, by his emphasis upon the ' merit ' of faith,
has led us to a point at which his doctrine (obscured though
it is by arguments which appeal to us little if at all) is seen
to have its roots deep in the New Testament.   Faith is
simply one aspect of the Christian's attempt (sometimes

conscious, sometimes unconscious) to please and serve God. The centurion, the blind man of Jericho, the Syro-Phœnician woman, and all the others whose faith the Lord commends, did not believe because they regarded faith as the necessary preliminary to a miracle ; they expected miracles because they believed. Nor did they ' believe ' as the result of an inevitable chain of argument. The same is true of Abraham, whose faith throughout the New Testament stands as a pattern of Christian faith. The confession of faith—whatever form it took in each case—was called out spontaneously as one part of the believer's committal and surrender of his soul to God. So it is with St. Thomas. Tendencies we have already noticed in modern thought have served to obscure this strictly evangelical truth, and faith has become no more than a necessary (or, as some at least would have us think, a superfluous) preliminary to the Christian life. St. Thomas knew that it was far more than a preliminary. It is true that it will not remain ' in patria,' [1] but that is merely because it will be superseded by the vision of God which is its goal. But in this life it is all-important, not in the low guise of a mere preparatory attitude of mind, but as a constant drawing near to God with the understanding. The daily ' act of faith ' of the Christian, his daily saying of the creed, can be and ought to be as much an act of homage to God as any other form of service or of worship. It is surely true to say that in this matter St. Thomas has taken us back to something which is very much of the essence of the gospel, but which a transient phase of anti-intellectualism in religion has all too unhappily obscured.

However this may be, we cannot avoid the conclusion that this conception of faith makes necessary those two principles noticed at the outset of this chapter. If faith is an essential and integral part of drawing near to God,

[1] i. 2, q. 67, a. 3.

no man can be ' saved '—that is brought wholly to God—
without it ; and indeed it will be difficult for a man to
advance far on the road to salvation, if his mind is not set
towards this task of finding, appropriating and affirming
all that is true of God, as a part of the loving homage and
honour which he pays to God. Nor is it more than barely
conceivable that such a desire to honour God and render
Him the free and loyal service of the understanding can be
inspired by anything less than the conviction that ' He
is, and is a rewarder of them that seek Him.' You cannot
easily honour a First Cause, nor offer undistracted devotion
to a pantheon of divinities. One God, and that one of such
a kind that man can enter into personal relations with
Him—the ' reward ' of ' friendship '—is the least that will
inspire faith in this sense. We may reject St. Thomas's
conception of faith if we will, even after we have stripped
it of its accidents and reached its essentials. In rejecting
it we shall reject something, as was suggested above, very
closely akin—for all its differences of thought and expression
—to the teaching of the New Testament. But if we accept
it, with all its delicate balance between reasonableness and
praiseworthiness—both of them characteristics dear to
God—we must give serious weight to these two corollaries,
that without such faith no man can as yet have drawn
very near to God or to the salvation which being near to
God implies ; and that the lowest thought about God
that will inspire this faith is the thought that ' He is and is
a rewarder of them that seek Him.' [1]

[1] To complete the argument of the above section, it would be necessary to discuss the scholastic corollary that even this minimum of
certainty (that ' God is, and is a rewarder ') is not attainable by the unaided human reason—the position which made it impossible for the
Church to accept the theory of ' fides late dicta.' The point need not
detain us however. Modern thought as a whole, so far from maintaining
the contrary, hesitates to accept even St. Thomas's confident assertion
of the demonstrability of the First Cause ; and even though the latter
were found to be provable, it would, as St. Thomas and Soto pointed out,
be less than the minimum required to generate faith.

## V

It was just this harmony also which St. Thomas maintained between the reasonableness and the praiseworthiness of faith which made it so difficult for him to accept 'invincible ignorance,' in the later sense, (or, as he would say, 'blindness' and 'dulness,') as an excuse for refusal to assent to the faith on the part of those to whom it had been propounded. Such a refusal must take one of two forms—either, 'I cannot see that what you allege to be true of God can be believed without doing violence to reason'; or, 'I can see that it *might* be believed without doing violence to reason, but I have yet to find a motive for believing it.' The former of these two objections could hardly be accepted by St. Thomas without denying the reasonableness of the faith. There may be here and there a man so childish in mind that not even the simplest argument will appeal to him. But such a man is an exception ; the mass of men are capable of grasping ordinary reasonableness. And 'reasonableness,' as applied to faith, must mean 'universal' or 'ordinary' reasonableness—a reasonableness that every reasonable man will see. A reasonableness which appeals to the elect and highly educated alone is something too precious and isolated to suffice as a basis for a faith which is to be world-wide. The second objection is as fatal. It implies that a man has no instinct moving him towards his supernatural end—that vision and service of God which is the only ultimate motive, as of the other theological virtues, so too of faith. This, again, may be true of a few degraded beings who have wholly or almost wholly stifled the longing for God which, to St. Thomas, is the inalienable heritage of every man ; it cannot be true of the mass of men. So to admit the plea of ' invincible ignorance ' in anything more than the extreme minority of men is to deny *either* the reasonableness of

faith (and consequently its praiseworthiness as well) *or*
the inherent Godward tendency of man.  And neither of
these alternatives could be accepted by the author of the
' Summa Theologica ' and the ' Summa contra Gentiles.'

Shift the balance ever so little ;—make faith more or
less ' reasonable ' than St. Thomas did ;—and the plea of
' invincible ignorance,' on behalf of those who having heard
the faith cannot accept it, is at once wholly unobjectionable.
No doubt Victoria (with Vasquez and de Lugo) did something to popularise the excuse by transferring responsibility from the hearer to the preacher, and suggesting that,
' sufficient ' proposition being necessary in every case, no
proposition could be considered ' sufficient ' which did
not in fact carry conviction with it.  But the real reason
why the doctrine of ' invincible ignorance ' in its new and
extended form established itself so readily, is that St.
Thomas's greatest disciples were not able to retain the
balance between the reasonableness and the ' voluntariness '
of faith.  Whilst rendering lip-service to all his characteristic doctrines, they in fact denied one or other of the two
complementary aspects of faith which he laboured to
establish.  That they did so unconsciously, and with no
intention other than that of building on his foundations,
need not be doubted ; but the fact remains that ' faith ' to
them was a different thing from what it was to him.

Thus Suarez, in the course of his discussion of the motive
of faith, asks whether ' this motive ' (the truth of God and
the fact of revelation) is known by the light of nature or
supernaturally ? [1]  St. Thomas's position is clear—at the
beginning of all faith there are reasoned and certain judgments of *fact*, however narrow in extent ; and among these
judgments are two that establish the motive of faith—a
judgment that ' God is veracious,' and a judgment that
' such and such a thing has been revealed.'  It is true that

[1] *de fid. theol.*, iii. 6, n. 1.

sometimes he limits the content of the judgment about God to a demonstration merely of the *credibility* of His existence and truth, as distinct from the *fact*. This however does not affect his general position that ' faith is born of knowledge,' although it reduces the amount of precedent ' knowledge,' in certain cases, to a minimum. The opposing point of view, that faith is founded only upon prior faith, Suarez clearly sees to involve a ' vicious circle ' : ' I believe that God is a Trinity because He asserts it ; I believe His assertion, because He is veracious ; I believe He is veracious because (again) He asserts it ' (n. 2). Nevertheless, he himself adopts this point of view, and alleges that the infallibility of God, as the ' first truth ' upon which all faith is based, must itself be embraced by faith (n. 4). It may not even be accepted as *proved* on the grounds that others in a responsible position hold it, ' as we believe that Rome exists (though we have not been there) on the authority of those who have been there.' His only explicit reason for the assertion is the scholastic one that an ' assent of a higher order cannot be founded on an assent of a lower order, nor can a greater certainty be built upon a less ' (n. 6). This we may admit in principle ; though the obvious reply is that St. Thomas has not made a distinction between ' higher ' and ' lower ' orders, but between two different kinds of assent. In a later passage [1] Suarez argues in the same way that the fact of revelation must be believed, and not merely *known* (if ' known ' at all) as a preliminary and part of the full Christian faith, though here the distinction is designated by other technical terms.[2] But nowhere does he face the difficulty which he himself has raised—that such a process must be a vicious circle leading nowhere.

De Lugo, on the other hand, though his argument is

---

[1] *de fid. theol.*, iii. 12.
[2] ' Fides acquisita ' and ' fides divina.'

obscure, tends to regard the act of faith as a piece of discursive reasoning based on two self-evident propositions.
To him the ' evidentia signa ' are beyond contradiction the
voice of God, intuitively recognised as such. ' My parents,
my masters, my reading and my whole acquaintanceship
with all these things, which come to me as immediate
knowledge, are as it were the voice of God, by which,
mediately and in a fashion, He has deigned to speak with
me. And so when books and preachers have made known
to me sufficiently the content of faith, it is as though God
Himself were dealing with me and telling me of that faith.' 1
I perceive intuitively that God is veracious and that what
He says is to be believed ; I hear by direct perception that
He says to me, ' This is so.' I conclude therefore syllogistically, ' Then I must believe it.' The appeal of this
conception need not be denied, but it is lacking in lucidity.
Above all we want to ask, ' How do you know that the
various channels by which the faith comes to you are
collectively the voice of God ? Is it by an act of faith ?—
If so, your doctrine is liable to the same criticism as that of
Suarez.2 Or is it a self-evident truth ? Then indeed your
faith is reasonable enough—but is it not either *too* reasonable and so not praiseworthy ; 3 or else (once again) founded
on something undemonstrable, and so no more than the
issue of an infinite regress ? '

It seems probable that the motive which lay behind these
speculations was the attempt to evade the very obvious
criticism to which St. Thomas had laid himself open—that
neither the truth, nor even the credibility, of the ' motive '

---

1 *de virt. fid. div.*, i. 7.
2 It seems clear, from de Lugo's incisive criticism of Suarez on this
point (*de virt. fid. div.*, i. 6–8 ; x. 2), that he did *not* himself accept this
alternative.
3 Because no more than the necessitated conclusion of a piece of
discursive reasoning—i.e. syllogistically, (1) ' All that God says is true ' ;
(2) ' God says such and such things ' ; (3) ' Therefore these things are
true.'

of faith can after all be proved by demonstrative reasoning. We can scarcely avoid the conviction that the faith of which St. Thomas wrote was, in the main, the faith of the educated and orthodox philosopher of his own day, confident in the certainties of human reasoning ; the faith of the plain man he ignored. Suarez and de Lugo are interested in the plain man, and both recognise that he very rarely ' has the demonstration ' of the existence and veracity of God and the fact of revelation ; and that often he may legitimately doubt whether even their credibility has been established. Suarez therefore makes him embrace the preambles by a prior act of faith ; de Lugo, as self-evident truths. Thus faith may yet flourish, even where no prior truths are thought of as proved certainties of reason. Fuller discussion would be necessary to criticise the two writers effectively, but one or two points are clear. (1) Both writers are emphasising, what St. Thomas also held but did not emphasise so much, the element of immediacy in the act of faith—the fact that, when all that can be said for its reasonableness has been said, there still remains at its very core something inexplicable and undemonstrated to which assent is given. (2) De Lugo's position is logically sounder than that of Suarez : it avoids the vicious circle. (3) Yet de Lugo's position would not satisfy St. Thomas, because it appears to take away from faith that ' voluntary ' element on which he laid so much stress, by representing it as an act of discursive reasoning from self-evident premisses. (4) As a matter of fact, though it takes away this element, it does not in any way affect the praiseworthiness of faith, which depends not upon its ' voluntariness,' as St. Thomas thought, but upon the desire to serve God in which it originates, and the heroic lives to which it gives birth. This, however, de Lugo did not recognise, and he attempted to restore the voluntariness of faith by difficult and devious arguments which only complicate his system further. But we need not follow up these by-ways of controversy, for it is plain now why Suarez and de Lugo could admit invincible ignorance of the faith in its widest sense, though St. Thomas could not. Base faith upon a prior act of faith, or upon a proposition self-evident to you, and you have no answer to the man who says ' I cannot believe as you can,' or ' I cannot see the self-evidence to which you appeal.' He and you belong to different worlds of thought. You cannot appeal to demonstrability if you have gone behind demonstration. All you can do is to agree to disagree ; and that is in effect what Suarez and de Lugo did with the heathen and the heretic.

And it must be admitted, that, with all their faults, Suarez and de Lugo were taking into account something of essential importance which St. Thomas had in the main ignored—the fact namely that Christian faith is more often called upon to struggle against reason, or to take a leap in the dark, than to accept the dictates of reason as proved and certain preliminaries in every way conformable to the faith. So much can be asserted, in dependence upon the facts of Christian experience, without in any way denying that for *some* (though not for as many as St. Thomas thought) the preambles or motives of faith can be demonstrated by sufficient reason ; or that in the end reason and faith must agree. Modern Roman Catholic theologians criticise their systems ;[1] but the criticism seems only to touch the point that in the *act of belief itself* there is not involved a conscious reference (discursive or otherwise) to the previous tenets of the existence and authority of God and the fact of revelation.[2] Of these tenets themselves such modern

---

[1] *E.g.* Billot, *de virt. infus.*, i. 292–298 ; Pesch, *Compend. Theol. Dogm.*, iii. 256.

[2] See especially Billot's analogy of the locomotive, *op. cit.*, p. 302, and compare J. H. Newman, *Grammar of Assent*, p. 167.

writers require that there should be a ' certain knowledge ' [1];
but they allow that the plain man may be content with a
' relative ' certainty. On this point, as we have seen, St.
Thomas was far from clear. ' Faith is born from knowledge '
was all that he cared to assert ; yet it may be suggested
that he would not have considered a ' relative certainty '
as the full equivalent of ' scientia.' Still, if the plain man's
faith is to stand good in the eyes of theology, either a precedent act of faith, or an immediate intuition (which may
be mistaken), or a ' relative certainty ' must be admitted.
There can be no doubt that true Christian faith, in the
sense of Abraham's or the Syro-Phœnician woman's, is
often found together with much intellectual hesitation and
uncertainty ;—hesitation and uncertainty crushed down
indeed by the act of faith, but overcome neither by that
nor by the arguments of reason. It is to this fact that
Suarez and de Lugo appeal. ' I am certain that God is
true and has revealed this truth ' is common to them and
St. Thomas. But whereas *he* would have added ' because
I have clear and convincing demonstration of His existence
and veracity,' *they* belong to a modern world which is
more disposed to add ' although many serious and weighty
reasons can be urged on the other side,' or ' although reason
does not seem to help much either way.' The modern world
may be wrong in its outlook, but it is the world with which
we have to deal ; and even if Suarez's ' prior faith ' and de
Lugo's ' immediate intuition ' are brought more into line
with official Thomism by the formula of ' relative certainty,'
St. Thomas's confident assertion of the triumph of reason
in the preambles is gone. And when it has gone ' faith '
is seen to be—often if not always—a little less reasonable
than he supposed it ; and ' invincible ignorance ' comes
once more to its own.

---

[1] ' Certa notitia,' Billot, *op. cit.*, 310 *sqq.*

## VI

The Vatican Council retained all the old Thomist language, emphasising the reasonableness and ' voluntariness ' of faith with an assurance no less definite than his.[1] But it did not in any way reject the humanised doctrine of the inculpable ' ignorance ' of the heretic and the heathen who in good faith would not accept the faith. It had, however, to face a further problem—that of positive and considered doubt on the part of Catholics. A German theologian, George Hermes († 1831), had maintained the thesis that the basis of all theological investigation should be ' positive doubt ' as to every article of faith. Not only did he assert that he himself had ' been faithful in the most conscientious way to his purpose of doubting everywhere as long as was absolutely possible,' but added that for future teachers of theology no other course was possible. ' They must learn that they know nothing, in order that they may seek knowledge more diligently ; they must have penetrated the inmost recesses of the labyrinth of doubt, that they may be able to offer themselves as companions to those who doubt, through all the intricacies of their wanderings.' [2]

This theory was condemned by Gregory XVI in a brief of the year 1835,[3] which Pius IX thought it wise to confirm. But the Council, in drawing up its constitutions and canons as to faith, recurred to the matter. After a clear definition of the indefectibility of faith as a virtue, it concluded with the words : ' And so the condition of those who by the celestial gift of faith have adhered to the Catholic truth is utterly different from that of those who, led by human opinions, follow a false religion ; for those who have received

---

[1] Sess. iii. *pass.* (Denz.-Bann., 1781–1820).

[2] Quoted from the authors of the first schema of the Constitution, Billot, *de virt. infus.*, i. 321.

[3] Denz.-Bann., 1618–1621.

K

the faith under the auspices of the Church can never have any just cause for changing their faith, or calling it back into doubt again.'[1] This seems at first sight definite and final ; but commentators on the Vatican decrees saw that it could scarcely be reconciled with the immunity from blame given to heathen and heretics who refused to believe in good faith. The same doubt might strike the Catholic when he came to years of reflection ; was he to be denied what in no metaphorical sense can be called the benefit of the doubt ? So Granderath[2] and Vacant[3] explain the *just* cause to mean an *objectively* just cause ; and maintain that the Council did not express any opinion on the action of those who, in all good conscience, find themselves unable to continue in the faith in which they have been educated, and so without formal or pertinacious heresy secede from the Church. The authors of the schema put before the Council had admitted as much.[4]

Later theologians accept this gloss on the decrees, with of course all due caution. ' Is it possible,' writes Pesch, ' for a man without formal heresy to leave the Church for a sect ? The possibility may be granted in the abstract. A person who lives under conditions unfavourable to the Church and favourable to a sect might perhaps, if he himself were only moderately instructed in Catholic doctrine, and neglected the means of getting better education and greater divine grace, allow his mind gradually to become more and more obscured until he no longer saw the duty of remaining in the Church, and passed over to the sect without a formally heretical spirit.'[5]  But Pesch continues :

---

[1] *Conc. Vat.*, Sess. iii.; *Const. de fide*, c. 3 (Denz.-Bann., 1794).  Cf. canon 6, *de fid.* (Denz.-Bann., 1815).

[2] *Constitutiones Concilii Vaticani explicatae* (1892), p. 61.

[3] *Études Théologiques sur les Constitutions du Concile du Vatican* (1895), ii., nn. 731-737.

[4] Quoted Tanquerey, *Synops. Theol. Mor.*, ii. 381.

[5] Pesch, *Compend. Theol. Dogm.*, iii. 262.  Cf. Tanquerey, *Synops. Theol. Dogm. Spec.*, i. 52.

' It would not seem possible to admit that anyone who had ever embraced Catholic truth by an act of faith could be guilty of such defection without sin. . . . One can fail and lose grace by many sins, even sins against faith, which are not formal heresy or infidelity . . . and so finally reduce oneself to a state of mind in which perseverance in the Catholic faith is morally impossible. This would be sin, grave sin, and that against faith ; but it would not be formal heresy.' Tanquerey [1] is even less emphatic. He would leave to ' more expert theologians ' the decision whether ' an uninstructed Catholic who falls among rationalists can lose his faith in the supernatural order without grave sin ' ; but he is equally clear that he need not be guilty of formal heresy.

These admissions, no doubt, are made with a degree of caution which Anglicanism would find a little un- necessary. The doctrine of the infallibility of the Papal authority is far-reaching, and its limitations as yet uncertain. Indeed Roman theologians themselves are not absolutely unanimous on the point.[2] But the force of the admissions is clear. There may be sin in secession from the Church on grounds of conscientious inability to believe or conform —that is for God to judge—but it need not be the grave sin of formal heresy, and involve inevitable loss of ultimate salvation. Invincible ignorance [3] once more throws its cloak over the suspected sinner, this time in the matter of conscientious doubt.

There remains, however, one obstacle which, in the Roman communion at all events, it would seem that the doctrine of invincible ignorance cannot overcome. It has

---

[1] *loc. cit.* Cf. his *Synopsis Theol. Mor.*, ii. 381, 382 : ' If I may give my opinion in this difficult matter, it is that no one can secede from the faith *once adopted* without some fault, if only of imprudence.'

[2] Thus Billot, *de virt. inf.*, i. 321 : ' de Catholicis *absque ulla restrictione* asserendum est, nullam eos habere posse justam causam etc.'

[3] The phrase is actually used in the ' Schema ' in this connection.

provided both for the inculpability of heathen and heretic who cannot accept the faith, and for at all events a relative degree of beatitude for them in the future life. It has provided, hesitatingly and with strict limitations, for the Catholic who finds himself with a subjectively just reason for seceding from the Church. But it has not provided for the Catholic who cannot accept one article of belief or conform with one principle of conduct, while able and glad to retain his hold upon the remainder. And such an one cannot be provided for so long as the doctrine of the infallibility of the Church remains in force, if the proposition or principle, from which belief or conformity is withheld, has been laid down on the conditions which provide for the exercise of that infallibility. To reject any such article so propounded is to reject the further article of the infallibility of the Church ; and though (as we have seen) proposition by the infallible authority of the Church is not an *essential* prerequisite for the belief of any article of the faith, it is the normal one.[1] The conscientious rejection of any one clause in the creed (let us say) is tantamount therefore in all normal cases to the rejection of the whole ; for the whole, like the part, has reached the Christian on the authority of the Church. The individual may indeed secede from the Church without the formal sin of heresy ; but his position, if he remained in it in a state of invincible ignorance (in the wide sense) towards one or more of its principal tenets, would be utterly equivocal.

This was quite definitely stated by St. Thomas in relation to the problem, ' Whether a person who disbelieves one article of the faith can have " fides informis " as to the other articles ? '[2]  It is true that the question as propounded by the objector refers definitely to heretics ; but the principle stated in reply is universal.  ' A heretic who

[1] Cf. Pesch, *op. cit.*, iii. 245 ; *supra*, p. 111.
[2] *S.T.*, ii. 2 ; q. 5, a. 3.

disbelieves one article of the creed,' St. Thomas says, 'retains neither "formed" nor "unformed" faith. . . . The "formal object" of faith is the "first truth" according as it is manifested in holy Scripture and the teaching of the Church, which proceeds from the first truth. So anyone who does not adhere to the teaching of the Church (which proceeds from the first truth manifested in Scripture) as to an infallible and divine rule, lacks the habitude of faith. He may hold that which is of faith, but he does not hold it by faith; just as a man has an opinion <only>, and not knowledge, when he holds a conclusion intellectually without having the means of proving it. . . . So a heretic who pertinaciously disbelieves one article of faith is not prepared to follow in all things the doctrine of the Church,[1] . . . therefore he has not got faith in the remaining articles, but rather an opinion arising out of his own choice.' Modern Roman theologians merely re-echo this statement.[2]

It would seem therefore that, at the point where the clash between law and conscience is most acute, the doctrine of invincible ignorance can offer no help. A man must either secede from the Church, or, if he remains within, conform. Almost all the cases of conscience created by

[1] He adds here the parenthesis : ' If he is not pertinacious, he is not a heretic, but in error.' This is quite orthodox, but does not help us—for ' error ' here (as always in St. Thomas) is used in the strictest sense ; and to refuse to accept correction by the Church would at once create pertinacity. The doctrine is endorsed with emphasis by Cardinal Newman, *Grammar of Assent*, p. 191.

[2] Billot, *op. cit.*, i. 348 ; Pesch, *op. cit.*, iii. 263, etc. Tanquerey, however, at all events in one passage, appears to contemplate the possibility of a Catholic being in invincible ignorance (in the widest sense) as to *one* article of the faith, and orthodox as to the remainder. See *op. cit.*, ii. 382 : ' If anyone doubt about an article of faith out of ignorance, and is ready to accept it *as soon as he recognises* (' statim ac noverit ') that it is revealed truth, he commits no sin of heresy ; but his sinfulness is determined by the degree to which his ignorance is vincible or invincible.' Everything here turns on the meaning of ' recognises.' If it merely means ' is informed on the infallible authority of the Church,' the passage simply echoes the position stated above in the text ; if it means anything more than that, it suggests a liberalism in advance of anything here quoted.

the interplay of the 'internal' and 'external norms' of truth and right action are cases in which an individual wishes to remain within the Church on terms of *general* conformity, but without binding himself finally to all the present, and still less to all the future, rulings of the Church. In the Roman communion such a position would seem to be impossible.  Is it the same in the Church of England?

# CHAPTER V

## CONFORMITY

### I

FOR English Churchmen, at all events, the problem of conformity presents itself most acutely in the matter of faith and doubt. Various causes contribute to this result. In the first place, it seems true to say that the dictates of Christianity in the matter of conduct do not, as a rule, meet with such violent opposition as is aroused by some at least of the articles of the creed. There may indeed be precepts of the Church whose relevance to the development of the spiritual life appears at best to be remote ; there are certainly others which have from time to time incurred criticism as being ill-advised, vexatious, or unduly burdensome. But there seem to be few, if any, which actually revolt the conscience of a would-be Christian, and impel him to testify against them as fundamentally iniquitous and immoral. Among the articles traditionally held to be ' of faith ' by Christians, on the other hand, are some which to many seekers after truth appear not merely unproven but definitely untrue ; to which, therefore, they cannot in conscience extend even the minimum of assent. Again, the doctrine which we have been considering, of the necessity for salvation of (at all events) a definite measure of faith, insists more explicitly upon conformity than does any corresponding precept in the moral sphere. It is true that mortal sin, in Catholic theology, deprives the soul of sanctifying grace and so (until a change of heart occurs) of the chance of salvation ; but there is no such authoritative tabulation of mortal sins as there is of the necessary articles of belief. Everything depends far more upon the circumstances of the individual case, the gravity of the matter, the degree of advertence, and so forth ; the barrier erected between the dissident and his salvation is, in all these respects, less rigid.   And even if it be urged that the first principles of the ' natural law ' (assuming these to be certainly ascertainable) demand no less absolute conformity than the necessary articles of faith, it may yet be replied that the conscience of every reasonable being gives him, by hypothesis, knowledge of the natural law, and impels him to obey it ; whilst his ' natural reason ' does not in the same way lead him to a knowledge of the ' revealed truth ' necessary for salvation.

Furthermore, whilst *ex animo* acceptance of the Church's ruling is ideally no less desirable in the matter of conduct than in the matter of faith, a reluctant and unwilling conformity to the ' law ' in outward conduct is at least always possible, and may even in certain circumstances be laudable.   Unwilling belief, on the other hand, if not actually (as St. Augustine held [1]) a psychological impossibility, is at all events on the Thomist doctrine of faith [2] a contradiction in terms ; whilst outward conformity in matters of faith, if combined with inward incredulity, so far from being laudable, is the merest hypocrisy.   We may on occasion—as, for example, to avoid offending the weaker brother—do something other than that which we consider ideally right ; but we cannot conscientiously for that reason, or for any other, either believe or profess to believe anything other than that which we consider to be true.

Grounds such as these may provide some justification for approaching the problem of conformity (as previous chapters have done) mainly from the side of faith.   It is

---

[1] *de spir. et lit.*, 31 (54).          [2] *Supra*, p. 99.

on that side that the gravest difficulties must arise. Even on that side the doctrine of invincible ignorance appears to provide a practicable solution in most cases of conflict between law and conscience ; it has so far failed us only where the Christian is conscientiously unable to accept the law in one particular, though willing enough to conform in other respects. This difficulty, however, though we reached it by a consideration of the question of faith, is obviously no less crucial in matters of conduct. Where the Church has felt so strongly on a point of morals as authoritatively to define that the Christian *ought* to behave in such and such a way, a believer who resolutely refuses to comply must be in the same case as one who rejects any part of the *lex credendi*. We may therefore at this stage leave the more particular problem of faith, and return to the general question ; and as attempts to reach a solution by way of the doctrine of ignorance appear for the moment to have failed, it becomes necessary to revert to the subject of ' law.'

For reasons briefly enumerated in the first chapter, it was inevitable that the Christian Church should enter upon its career not only as a society which recognised in law one of its guiding principles, but as a society which had in its possession from the first no mean system of laws. The system needed codification, of course : some of its most Judaistic elements had to go ; the specific contribution of the teaching and example of the Lord was bound to redistribute the emphasis throughout the whole. But from the first it was a system, and early documents such as the ' Didaché ' and the ' Pastor ' show that as a system it was not uncongenial. To oppose to that respect for law, which marked Jewish, Stoic and imperial thought alike, a merely individualistic gospel, would have been a revolution such as, rightly or wrongly, never entered the mind of any primitive Christian.

Other circumstances, again, made it as inevitable that

the Church should continue for centuries as a law-wielding society.   The need for organisation, order, and unity, in face first of all of persecution and then of heresy ; the same need, later, as a bulwark against the chaos into which the Empire broke up, compelled the leaders of the Church to exercise an authority as vigilant as, if not more vigilant than, at any previous time.   Christianity has sometimes been thought of as, in essence, a purely individualistic religion in which each man, guided by the Spirit of God, is a law to himself ; but even if the truth and adequacy of such a conception could be established it would still have to be conceded that, humanly speaking, the Church never had a chance of realising this ideal.   The force of circumstances must have been, from the very outset, too strong for it ; tradition, assimilation, persecution, heresy, and anarchy would together have forced it into some such mould as that which it actually took—the mould of an organised and disciplined Church.   But as a matter of fact this development, so far from being foreign to the genius of Christianity, appealed to one at least of its most treasured convictions.   Modern theology is practically unanimous in the conclusion that Christianity is by nature, as it was from the outset in fact, a consciously social religion, conferring privileges and imposing duties upon its adherents as members of a corporate body. If this is true, it is hardly surprising that the idea of an organised Church, whose function in part at least was to maintain those privileges and enforce those duties by an authoritative system of law, met with little serious opposition in the early age of Christianity.

To describe the progressive organisation of the Church on this basis would involve a history of the canon law from its earliest beginning, at least to the completion of the ' Corpus.'  It is sufficient, however, to have noticed that such a development was not merely forced upon the Church by external circumstance, but was inherent in the genius of

Christianity. The Church as the new Israel—the Church as
the Body of Christ—the Church as the Temple of God—
the Church as the terrestrial representative of a celestial
Kingdom—these and many other phrases indicate clearly
this social character of Christianity as the New Testament
writers contemplated it.    There may be all kinds of disputes
and questionings as to the authority which is to lay down
the law in such a society, and as to the conditions on which
the law must be regarded as ' just ' or ' binding ' ; but that
there must *be* such an authority, and that it must legislate
and administer, never comes into question at all.    The
question for the Church to decide (apart from those of the
seat of authority, and the conditions with which its laws, to
be duly promulgated, must comply) was always and only
the question of the rights of conscience as against law.

A ' certain ' conscience, as we have seen, has always an
inalienable right as against law wherever the two conflict.
It need not, however, connote complete inculpability unless
the conditions of genuine invincibility [1] are satisfied ; it
may even—in the Roman communion at all events—involve
its possessor in banishment from the Church, if its clash with
law is on a major point of faith or morals.    But quite apart
from these important limitations, it is clear that often
enough conscience is ' doubtful,' and lays down no certain
injunction ;  often it is ' perplexed,' seeing before it two
courses, each of them equally objectionable or unobjectionable ;  and *at all times* it requires careful and constant
education in the principles of Christian conduct, lest its
'certainties' become the certainties of callousness or licence.
What are the rights or claims of duly promulgated ecclesiastical law at such times as these ?

On this subject two very contrary views have been held.
The first was that of Gerson—in this matter, as in others, a
precursor of modern liberalism.    To him ecclesiastical law

---

[1] *Supra*, p. 34.

was only binding in so far as it admittedly and patently applied the principles of the natural and divine law.   Canon law, therefore, ' induces no obligation, but merely explains or sets forth something which is inferred with certainty or probability from revealed principles.' [1]   ' The omission of the canonical hours, the neglect of ecclesiastical fasts and generally of all statutes, rules, and canons, is never a mortal sin except in so far as it is found to be contrary to a divine precept ; and therefore only in so far as a given law has an admixture of divine precept, *but no farther*, is its breach a mortal sin.' [2]

This position, attractive though it may appear at first sight, would if pressed to its logical conclusion reduce the unity and order of the Church to a mere shadow.   The organisation of the Church in the New Testament may not be as complete as that of an army ; but it is certainly more complete and disciplined than that of a touring club.   It extends to more details than could conceivably be regarded as directly ordained by natural and divine law.   On the mere analogy of civil society, a Church which numbered among its members saints and sinners, wise and foolish,

---

[1] This is Suarez's summary (*de legg.*, iv. 17 ; cp. iii. 21) following Gerson verbatim.   Suarez gives a list of other writers (mainly pre-Tridentine) who appear to agree with Gerson.   Similar lists in Sanderson, *de obl. consc.*, v. 6 ; Bellarmine, *de laicis*, iii. 9 ff.   The position of Calvin and Luther (see E. C. Wood, *Regal Power of the Church*, 39 ff.) may be compared with that of Gerson.

[2] Gerson, *Tract. de vit. spir. an.*, lect. 4, coroll. 4.   The difference between Gerson and Suarez is (as the latter partly grasped) not so great in fact as appearance.   In dependence upon Aquinas, Suarez saw in the law of nature and the positive divine law a norm of greater sanctity than any human law (even the ecclesiastical), to which human law, to oblige in conscience, was bound to conform.   Gerson's position may be summed up as : ' Only those laws oblige which are seen to enshrine the principles of natural or divine law ' ; Suarez's : ' No law obliges in conscience which is seen to conflict with natural or divine law.'   See Aquinas, *S.T.*, i. 2, q. 96, a. 4 ; Suarez, *de legg.*, i. 9 ; iii. 22 ; and cp. Figgis, *From Gerson to Grotius*, pp. 7, 8 (on St. Thomas, quoting from Lord Acton, ' Not the devil but St. Thomas Aquinas was the first Whig '), 57 (on Gerson, etc.), 175 (Suarez and the Jesuits).

adults and children, the eager and the lukewarm, the normal
and the abnormal, could never safeguard the rights of one
member against another by enunciating a few general principles (however noble and inspiring in character) and leaving
the rest to the conscience or choice of the individual. It
may be urged that no more than this would be needed in a
Church made up wholly of zealous Christians ; but the
Church never has been, and apparently was never intended
to be, a home for zealots only ; nor, if it allowed itself to be
so, could it carry on its evangelistic and edificatory mission.
The discipline of conscience which is a necessary condition
of entry into the Church is admittedly a minimum ; in all
normal cases it requires to be reinforced and completed by
a discipline of conscience for those within the fold.

Considerations such as these, no doubt, led the great
majority of theologians to adopt a different and more
rigorous view. So far from regarding ecclesiastical laws as
purely advisory, expressing ways in which Christian experience has found it profitable to urge believers to direct
their lives, they held that, in every case except that of the
certain conscience, such laws have a claim to obedience
which cannot be disregarded except on pain of grave if not
mortal sin. The bare possibility that the Church may enact
something contrary to the natural or divine law is of course
allowed ; [1] in such a case the law is ' unjust ' and need not be
obeyed. But this exception is really covered by the doctrine
that a certain conscience abrogates, for a *particular* individual on a *particular* occasion, the promulgated law. Apart
from this, as St. Thomas says, ' just laws enacted by men
draw force to bind in the forum of conscience from the
eternal law from which they are derived, as is written in
Prov. viii. 15, *By me kings reign and princes decree justice.*' [2]

<hr/>

[1] *S.T.*, i. 2, q. 96, a. 4, ad 2, 3.
[2] *Ib.*, cf. ii. 2, q. 104, a. 6 ; q. 105. He is speaking of ' human ' law
in general—ecclesiastical and civil alike.

Suarez maintains at length that all ' civil law,' if just, binds in conscience,[1] even though its ' derivation ' from the law of nature may be so remote as to be incapable of demonstrative proof—as, for example, laws prohibiting the carrying of weapons after nightfall. Generically, such laws bind under pain of mortal sin,[2] though circumstances may lessen the degree of obligation.[3] Passing on then to canon law, he establishes without difficulty the principle that the Church has a ' more excellent ' claim upon conscience than the State.[4] Beyond all cavil, therefore, its law must oblige in conscience ; [5] though here again a breach of it is not necessarily and in all cases an act of mortal sin,[6] and its degree of obligation varies with the gravity of the matter, the form of the law, and the intention of the legislator. The Council of Trent naturally enough took the same point of view ; [7] indeed except for Gerson and his few supporters, there is no dissentient voice.

The leaders of post-Reformation Anglicanism took equally strong ground in their doctrine of the authority of the Church. We ' owe no less than childlike obedience to her that hath more than motherly power,' said Richard Hooker ; [8] and again : ' Such customs or rites as are publicly established demand approbation with good conscience.' [9] Jeremy Taylor is equally definite and even more detailed. ' If our Bishop,' he says in one of his examples,[10] ' in his precepts and sermons of chastity, command that the women go not to the public spectacles where are represented such things as would make Cato blush, and Tuccia have looser thoughts, they are bound, in conscience, to abstain from those impure societies.' There is here no essential difference of attitude

---

[1] *de legg.*, iii. 21.          [2] *Ib.*, 24.          [3] *Ib.*, 25–28.
[4] iv. 8. He quotes Ignatius, Ambrose, Chrysostom, etc. in support.
[5] iv. 17.                       [6] iv. 18.
[7] Sess. vii, can. 8, *de bapt.* (Denz.-Bann., 864) ; cf. Bellarmine, *disp. de summ. pont.*, iv. 16, etc.
[8] *Laws of Eccl. Polity*, v. 8.          [9] *Ib.*, v. 6.
[10] *Duct. Dub.*, III, iv, rule 4. Cp. Sanderson, *de obl. consc.*, prael. v. 22 ff., where objections are considered.

towards duly promulgated law (whether imposed by canon or by the ordinary) from that of the Schoolmen. And no other attitude, it must be conceded, is compatible with a recognition of the character of the Church either as a world-wide and evangelistic society, or as a society founded, sent out, and maintained by God.

Such an attitude is tantamount to a confession of the general indefectibility of the Church in matters of faith and morals ; for a body frequently liable to error could scarcely claim obedience ' in foro conscientiae,' however much it might enforce it ' in foro externo.' It is not, however, bound up with any doctrine of complete or actual infalli-bility. The former belief, rather than the latter, is the one which dominates the principle that ecclesiastical laws and formularies have an authoritative claim upon conscience which is only waived—and that no more than temporarily—when conscience is ' certain ' in an opposite sense. No one would be hardy enough to assert the infallibility of ecclesi-astical pronouncements in more than a relatively few in-stances of supreme importance, whereas it is clear that the writers just quoted regard the claim of law as authoritative even when enshrined in no more than an episcopal injunction. Again, the claim of law has been asserted at all times and in all branches of the Church, as also has the doctrine of general indefectibility ; whilst the doctrine of infallibility is a late and local growth. Its vestiges are to be seen indeed in Irenæus's reference to the ' charism of truth ' given to Bishops at their ordination ; [1] and in the attribution to them-selves of plenary inspiration by many of the councils. But as late as Augustine it was still held that the formularies even of general councils could be ' emended ' by later ones,[2]

---

[1] adv. haer., iv. 26, 2.

[2] de bapt. c. Don., ii. 3 (4). Cp. Ath., de Syn., 47 ; Apol. c. Arian., 2 (22)—the letter of Julius. Dr. Kidd (Thirty-nine Articles, p. 186) quotes from Bp. Collins, Authority of General Councils (Church Historical Society Lectures, ii. p. 167) : ' No such ideas of the finality of a General Council as are now current were then held in the Church.'

and that the Church's authority, though 'inaugurated by miracles, nourished in hope, and enlarged by love,' required also to be 'confirmed by age' and by universal 'consent' to keep men in her bosom.[1] The doctrine that the Church's legislation upon *conduct*, as well as her proclamation of the *faith*, is infallible, does not appear till the sixteenth century ; even Melchior Cano († 1560), who formulated it, confines its operation to 'res gravis et quae ad Christianos mores apprime conducat.'[2]

On the other hand, the doctrine of the general indefectibility and inerrancy of the Church, without any detailed theory as to its actual infallibility on special occasions, is of universal acceptance. It occurs so frequently in the patristic period that quotations would be entirely superfluous to illustrate it. The Schoolmen accept it without hesitation, though of course they go far also in the direction of curialist infallibility. Continental Reformers and Anglican divines are no less emphatic. William Palmer, in his 'Treatise on the Church of Christ'[3] (a book which deserves to be remembered in the Church of England), cites a long list of authorities for both the Continental and the English post-Reformation communions[4] which, so far from showing any weakening towards the doctrine of indefectibility, go a long way towards asserting the infallibility of the councils accepted as œcumenical ; and his survey

---

[1] 'Vetustate formata,' *c. ep. Man.*, 4 (5).   Cp. Reuter, *Augustinische Studien*, 358.

[2] *de loc. theol.*, v. 5.   As a matter of fact, Antoninus of Florence († 1459) asserted the doctrine as a pious opinion, the denial of which would amount to heresy (*Summa*, p. iii, tit. 12, c. 8, § 2—on the inerrancy of the Church in canonisations).   He had a certain warrant for this in St. Thomas (*Quodl.*, ix, a. 16—on the same subject), though generally (e.g. *S.T.*, i. 2, q. 93, a. 3, ad 3, a. 4 ; q. 96, a. 1, ad 3 ; q. 105, a. 2, ad 8 ; ii. 2, q. 120, a. 1) St. Thomas denies the infallibility of human, and therefore of ecclesiastical, law.

[3] 3rd edition, London, 1842.

[4] Vol. ii., pp. 89–93.   The quotations are drawn from the Confession of Augsburg, Calvin, Chillingworth, Field, Hammond, Pearson, Bramhall, Tillotson, Bull.

concludes with the words : ' Scarcely any Christian writer can be found who has ventured actually to maintain that *the judgment of the universal Church, freely and deliberately given, with the apparent use of all means*, might in fact be heretical and contrary to the gospel.'

This, however, at once suggests an important difference between the Church of England and the Church of Rome in the matter of authority and conscience.  Whilst many Anglican writers assert the *de facto* infallibility (at all events in matters of faith) of the œcumenical councils of the un-divided Church, and might be prepared to admit the same doctrine of an undivided Church of the future, there is no official Anglican pronouncement on either of these points—except indeed one whose tendency as a whole is *against* any doctrine of infallibility.[1]  Still less is there any conception of an existing organ of infallibility to which appeal may at any time be made, and which is capable of altering the system of faith and morals at any moment by an *ex cathedra* pronouncement.  It follows, therefore, that the disability under which members of the Roman communion labour, and to which allusion was made at the end of the preceding chapter, does not affect the Church of England.  There may be reasons which justify the conclusion that an Anglican, who is conscientiously unable to accept or conform to one of the major articles of Christian faith and practice, cannot fairly claim to remain a member of his communion.  But the reason which operates in the Church of Rome—that nonconformity of this kind carries with it disbelief in the infallibility of the Church, and so throws doubt on *every* article of belief and rule of conduct—has no place in the Church of England.  Whatever reasons may be alleged to support the thesis that conformity in all important particulars is essential, this one cannot fairly be brought forward.

[1] Article 21 of 1563.

L

## II

Do the conditions of the Church of England, therefore, make it legitimate for a member of the body conscientiously to refuse conformity in any matter of weight, and still retain his membership with all its rights and privileges ? There is difference of opinion between Rome and Anglicanism, as on other questions of order, so on that of the seat of authority in the Church and the conditions of due promulgation of ecclesiastical law. That, however, does not affect the question. Nor does the difference we have just noticed on the subject of infallibility affect it, except negatively ; it removes one difficulty from the path, but does not mitigate any others there may be. In the matter of ecclesiastical authority as a whole there is, as we have seen, absolute unanimity between the two communions. What has to be decided, therefore, is the question whether (the doctrine of infallibility set on one side) the claim of authority can be fully satisfied by a Christian who accepts some articles proposed to him by authority, but conscientiously refuses to accept others. Is there still a place for him in the Church ?

We have to notice first of all a distinction of vital importance to our purpose. We have spoken hitherto as though the authoritative voice of the Church made itself heard only through duly promulgated law. But this is very far from being the case. Theologians and canonists unanimously agree that, on certain conditions, established custom has the force and authority of promulgated law.[1]

---

[1] Augustine, *Ep.* xxxvi. 2 : ' in his rebus de quibus nihil certi statuit Scriptura divina, mos populi Dei et instituta majorum pro lege sunt tenenda ' ; Tert., *de corona*, 3-5 (contrast *de virg. vel.* 1) ; Aquinas, *S.T.*, i. 2, q. 97, a. 3, etc. ; cp. ii. 2, q. 10, a. 12, in corp. ; Suarez, *de legg.*, viii, esp. c. 16 ; and commonly. For the same doctrine in the Church of England, cp. the 34th Article of Religion ; Jeremy Taylor, *Duct. Dub.*,iii. 4, rule 15 ; iii. 6, rule 6 ; R. Hooker, *Laws of Eccl. Polity*, v. 7, 65 ; and for Anglican canonists, Ayliffe, *Parergon* (1726), pp. 194–196 ; Gibson,

Custom can introduce, interpret, and even (at times) abrogate duly promulgated law. Both canonists and Schoolmen frankly admit this last point, which is of peculiar importance. The former looked back to a definite state- ment of Gratian [1]—' Some laws have to-day been abrogated by contrary custom . . . and because they have not received the approbation of general use, those who do not observe them are not thereby proved guilty of dis- obedience ' ;—and a vague phrase of Gregory IX [2]—' Long- standing custom, though of great authority, cannot be prejudicial to law, *unless it be reasonable and legitimately prescribed* ' (i.e. of a certain standing, etc.).  The moralists appealed to Aquinas, who admitted [3] that ' propter aliquam mutationem hominum ' a law might cease to have value, and a contrary custom duly abrogate it.  In such a case, the custom would have its inception in the actions of those upon whom the law pressed with undue severity ; and if their non-observance of the law were justified by the urgency of the case, the custom, though contrary to the law, would come into being without actual sin on the part of anyone.[4]  Suarez is not so certain that a custom contrary to law can be introduced without sin ; on the other hand, he extends the principle in a direction of profound import- ance by suggesting that a law even of the universal Church may be abrogated by a contrary custom in a particular province, diocese, or ' community ' ;—' for if in one of these " communities " a custom should prevail among the

---

*Codex Jur. Eccl. Angl.* (1761), Pref. xiii ; Int. Disc. xxvii ; tit. xli, c. 1 (on 25 Hen. VIII, c. 21) ; Stillingfleet, *Eccles. Cases*, p. i (*Works*, London, 1710, iii, pp. 708–710) ; p. ii, disc. i (*ib.*, pp. 754, 757).  Sanderson (in accordance with his general rigorism) has little to say about custom, and confines himself to pointing out its limitations as compared with law (*de obl. consc.*, iii. 21).  The *locus classicus* for the doctrine of the authority of custom was Basil, *de Spiritu Sancto*, 27 (66) : see *Corp. Jur. Can.*, c. 5, D. xi.

[1] *Corpus*, c. 3, D. iv. ; contrast D. xi, D. xii, *pass.*
[2] *Ib.*, c. 11, X. i. 4 ; cp. c. i. in Sext., i. 2.
[3] *S.T.*, i. 2, q. 97, a. 3.                    [4] q. 96, a. 6.

majority contrary to universal law, for that community
<the law> is abrogated (*derogatur*), even though for the
rest it remains intact.' [1]

It is here that the real difference between Rome and
Anglicanism in the matter of authority and the individual
conscience seems to show itself : and it is a vast and far-
reaching difference.   The genius of Rome has expressed
itself in extending to the utmost the sway of promulgated
law, at the expense of custom ; the genius of Anglicanism,
on the other hand, has taken the course of reducing the
domain of law to the barest possible minimum, and leaving
all else to the régime of custom.   Rome has a vast Codex
of 2414 canons continually augmented by decisions of the
congregations, tribunals, and offices ' by which the Roman
Pontiff is wont to forward the business of the Church,' [2]
and reinforced by the interpretations of moralists and
canonists which, though without the force of law, are yet
' of great value.' [3]   Anglicanism, on the contrary, has a
small body of operative ecclesiastical law ; [4]   and a large
body of traditional observation whose claim upon the
individual, unless and until defined by canon, is no more

[1] *de legg.*, vii. 18, 6.
[2] *Codex Jur. Can.* (Ben. xv.), can. 7.   Cp. cann. 246–264.
[3] Tanquerey, *Synops. Theol. Mor.*, ii. 176.
[4] The words ' ecclesiastical law ' are here used, in the strict sense, of
law duly enacted and promulgated by the competent legislative authority
of the Church, as distinct from statute law dealing with ecclesiastical
matters, which is of course purely civil law.   Of such statute law it seems
true to say (T. A. Lacey, *Handbook of Church Law*, p. 47) that ' secular
legislation affects Church law just so far as it is incorporated by custom into
the working system.   We must therefore enquire, in the case of each several
statute, whether it has in fact been so incorporated, or whether, on the
other hand, there has been sufficient resistance, active or passive, on the
part of the Christian Society to prevent the growth of a custom.'   Cp. *ib.*,
pp. 49, 159–162, 167 f. ; Gibson, *Codex*, i. p. xxix ; J. Johnson, *Ecclesiastical
Laws of the Church of England* (1720), Preface § 24.   But in respect of this
possibility of assistance, or ' interference,' on the part of the secular legis-
lature, Anglicanism is in no different position from that of the mediaeval
Church, or the post-Reformation Church of Rome.   See A. Tardif, *Histoire
des Sources du Droit Canonique*, pp. 261 ff.

and no less than the claim of custom.[1]  We may argue,
if we will, that the Anglican system is less or more efficient
than that of Rome, less or more reasonable, less or more
true to the example of the Lord and His Apostles.  But—
great though the difference of emphasis between the two
communions is—as far as the main principles of moral
theology and canon law in the West are concerned, what
can *not* be argued is that either system in any way ignores
those principles.  If the word ' Catholicism ' is taken to
mean a system of religion in which, among other things,
serious and conscientious deference is paid to whatever
has commanded the consensus of the main body of Christian
thought and practice in the past, then—in this matter at
least—Rome and Anglicanism must both be adjudged
' Catholic.'  Despite their wide divergences, they are no
more than variations (and variations at all events
logically permissible) of one and the same traditional
point of view—that namely which cedes to law and
custom respectively obligations upon the conscience of the
individual.[2]

The difference between Rome and England seems, therefore, to lie mainly in this, that whereas Rome recognises a
vast body of canon law and (in comparison) a relatively small

---

[1] It is commonly said (e.g. Wakeman, *History of the Church of England*,
220: cp. J. Johnson, *Eccles. Laws of Ch. of England*, p. xxix) that,
owing to the provision of the Act for the Submission of the Clergy
(25 Henry VIII, c. 20) that all existing canons, not contrary to the laws of
the realm or the king's prerogative, should be used and executed as before,
' large parts of the mediæval canon law form part of the ecclesiastical
law of England.'  But have they not, in the main, been abrogated for
conscience by desuetude ?

[2] We are happily not here concerned with the controversy as to
whether *in fact* custom in the mediæval Church had much avail against
contrary law.   This point was that at issue between Stubbs and Maitland,
who have recently found new champions respectively in Mr. Ogle (*Mediæval
Canon Law in the Church of England*), and Mr. Davis (*Canon Law in
England*, Proceedings of International Historical Congress, 1913).  But
the *principle* stated above, that custom can, in given circumstances,
introduce, interpret, and abrogate law, has never been disputed.

body of custom, Anglicanism has reversed the emphasis, and is more or less content with a small body of law and a very large degree of custom. What its friends call the ' inclusiveness ' of Anglicanism, and its enemies its ' chaos ' and ' indiscipline,' would appear to be not in any way a new system or discovery or way of life, but simply a justifiable variation of principles which the entire body of Western Christendom has for centuries recognised as inherent in the character of organised religion. But the fact that Anglicanism represents a unique variation of traditional principles means that we cannot accept blindfold from another communion—even though equally ' Catholic,' in the sense in which the word has just been used—corollaries appropriate enough in the circumstances of that communion. We must apply to the Anglican system the traditional formulæ which Christian experience has discovered, accepted, and elaborated ; but we need not be surprised if the new emphasis imported into the old forms by the post-Reformation Anglican Church produces results, in the application, different from those of other bodies. Such results, novel though they may appear, will be no less legitimate for all their novelty.

As we have already seen, the principal factor within the sphere of ordered Western Christianity, in determining the relation of the individual conscience to the authority of the Church in matters where a divergence is likely to occur, has always been a wise application of the doctrine of invincible ignorance. What Anglican theology has to decide are the methods by which that doctrine is to be applied to the specifically English variant of Church organisation, in which the authority of the community is expressed mainly through custom and only in a minor degree through law. Such methods, to be in general accord with the established mind of historic Western Christianity, will not be *new* methods. They will be the old methods applied

upon the old principles to circumstances which, though
new in themselves, are yet conformable to the recognised
canons of the Christian organisation.

### III

Dividing, then, 'what the Church teaches' into law
and custom (both binding upon conscience), and recog-
nising that in the English Church most of the 'teaching'
is the work of custom and only a little of 'law,' strictly
so called, can we allow the plea of invincible ignorance to
excuse from the guilt of sin, or from ecclesiastical penalties,
a Christian who fails, in one respect though not in others,
to conform to this teaching?   And first as to law.   Roman
moralists, as we have seen, admit the theoretic possibility
of complete conscientious divergence, without at all events
mortal sin, upon the part of the individual from the law and
teaching of the Church, even though he was baptised a
member of the Church.   We can all the more readily admit
this too, because our analysis suggested that the hesitations
of Roman writers were in the main due to the pressure of
the doctrine of infallibility.   That same pressure, however,
prevents the Roman theologian—as also it prevented St.
Thomas—from admitting the legitimacy of conscientious
nonconformity, *within* the Church, on particular points of
faith or morals.   In the Church of England it would appear
that this pressure does not exist, and consequently we may
fairly conclude that nonconformity on any one point (however weighty) may, at least in theory, be conscientiously
and without sin combined with loyal membership in other
matters.   The responsibility here, after all, rests with the
body : it has the legislative right to decide within what
limits nonconformity on the part of its members may still
be tolerated, and within those limits the individual would
appear to be free to follow the dictates of a *certain* conscience,

wherever it may lead him, without either the guilt of sin, or any moral obligation to dissociate himself from the community.

But every communion, and the Church of England not less than others, recognises that a point must come at which divergence in faith or morals from the promulgated law of the Church must be visited with penalties, of which the gravest is that of exclusion from the society and its privileges and benefits. And, clearly, no individual has the right to expect that divergence on his part, however conscientious it may be, should exempt him from penalties, whether previously enacted for such cases or specially enacted by legitimate authority for his case. Such a conclusion is obvious enough, even on Gerson's very attenuated theory of the obligation of law. Every society must have its rules, and persistent infringement of them after due warning (and in canon law, at all events, every penalty must be preceded by monition [1]) cannot go unvisited. It is, however, specially to be noticed that ecclesiastical penalties do not necessarily and in themselves touch the question of moral guilt ; [2] indeed, they are sometimes imposed where the individual is admittedly guiltless, or has fully and openly repented of his offence. Suarez instances the case of the person who has

---

[1] *Corp. Jur. Can.*, c. 15, C. xxiv, q. 3 ; c. 11, X. i. 2 ; *S.T.*, ii. 2, q. 11, a. 3, ad 6 ; *Conc. Trid.*, Sess. xxv. *de ref.*, c. 3 ; cp. *Codex Jur. Can.* (Ben. xv.), 2233, § 2.

[2] Thus it is a principle of canon law that ' circumstances which excuse from all guilt, or even from serious guilt, excuse also from all penalties . . . even *in foro externo, if the excuse can be made good* ('*evincatur*') *in the external forum*' (*Codex Jur. Can.*, 2218, § 2). This, as Noldin sees (*de poen. eccl.*, p. 20), implies that there *may* be cases where there is no guilt in conscience, but the fact of innocence cannot be proved to the satisfaction of authority. It will be recalled that even Abailard (*supra*, p. 8) admitted the legitimacy of the principle in question. It is obvious, however, that penalties should not be imposed unless moral culpability appears both grave and certain. Cp. *Corp. Jur. Can.*, cc. 41, 42, C. xi, q. 3 ; cc. 1, 23, X. v. 39 ; and Taylor, *Duct. Dub.*, iii. 4, rule 9, where the principle is crudely but effectively illustrated by the dictum, ' The judge is cruel and not just that puts a man to death with torments for spitting in his parlour.'

unwittingly lent himself to simoniacal practices. No moral blame can be attached to his action, for he was invincibly ignorant (in the narrower sense of the term) that he was infringing the law. Yet he might be called upon to suffer the penalty ' non ut poenam, sed, ut incommodum quod tolerandum est propter commune bonum, quia non sine causa imponitur,' or as ' remedium ad tollendas occasiones vel ad indecentiam vitandam.' The penalty is imposed ' non propter culpam sed propter ipsum factum.' [1]

It is unlikely that hard cases of this kind will occur in modern Anglicanism, where, wisely or unwisely, the imposition of penalties for ecclesiastical offences has been reduced to the lowest possible minimum. But in any case the principle holds good that the punishment of an offence by ecclesiastical censure has no *necessary* bearing whatever on the question of moral guilt. We have already accepted the conclusion that a member of the Church may, at the dictates of a certain conscience, refuse conformity even in a major question of faith and morals, and freely remain a member of the communion, so long as the penalty of exclusion has not been enacted for his case. We must agree, also, that even if he suffer the penalty of exclusion, or any lesser penalty, no certain inference as to his moral culpability can be drawn from the fact. He may still be in invincible ignorance, and so morally guiltless and capable of salvation. One further point remains to be added. No offender, even though aware that he has made himself liable to penalties, is required in conscience to take any step to secure the enforcement of those penalties, still less to put them into effect

[1] *de legg.*, v. 12 ; cp. Noldin, *de poen. eccl.*, p. 6 : ' Vindictive ' penalties (deposition, deprivation of benefice, etc.) are sometimes imposed ' pro delicto praeterito, etiam postquam <reus> resipuit.' *Ib.*, p. 21 : ' fieri potest ut quis per contritionem aut confessionem jam sit immunis a peccato, propter quod ab ecclesia punitur, quando ipsam poenam seu censuram de facto incurrit.' Cp. also Sanderson, *de obl. consc.*, prael. viii. 9.

himself.[1] Here as before, responsibility rests with the Church.

<h1 style="text-align:center">IV</h1>

But the vast majority of the principles of conduct recognised in the Church of England are, as we have seen, consuetudinary and not canonical ; and no penalty is attached to their neglect. Here it would seem that the doctrine of invincible ignorance, in that wide sense in which it is the equivalent of ' conscientious nonconformity,' is of immediate application. The parish priest finds himself continually face to face with the fact that principles, which he has constantly proclaimed as ' the invariable rule of the Church,' are questioned and neglected by many of his most devout parishioners, and that upon grounds which impartial consideration cannot but regard as strictly conscientious. As a general rule these principles are customary only, and no more ; they are not explicitly defined or accepted by the current law of the English Church ; and even though defined by laws which have never been officially repealed, may yet in many cases be thought of as abrogated by custom. Here the problem presents itself in a new form. Where a custom is rejected at the dictate of a ' certain ' conscience, moral guilt is only involved if the conscientious-ness is not genuinely invincible. But if conscience does

---

[1] Unless they be of the rare kind known as ' poenae latae sententiae ' (i.e. penalties designated in the law itself as *ipso facto* incurred by the offence). Even here the offender is not morally bound to put them into effect publicly until a special declaratory sentence has been issued for his case, nor privately if it would involve ' infamy ' of any kind, unless the offence is notorious. So *Corp. Jur. Can.*, c. 10, X. iii. 2 ; *Codex*, 2232, § 1. Cp. also T. A. Lacey, *Handbook of Church Law*, 27 : ' Excommunication is in some cases said to be incurred *ipso facto*. This means that the censure must be necessarily imposed by the spiritual judge when the fact of delinquency is brought to his notice. It does not mean that the censure is actually incurred without the public action of a competent judge. There must be a declaratory sentence, openly advertising both the offender and the faithful at large of the censure imposed.'

not proclaim with certainty against the custom, though it cannot *ex animo* and spontaneously accept it, what claim has the custom upon the individual then ? Must it be obeyed until conscience proclaims certainly against it ? Or may it be disregarded until conscience comes out certainly on its side ?

All depends here upon the definition of a ' legitimate ' custom ; for ' legitimate ' custom, by universal consent, obliges in all cases with the same force as promulgated law unless and until the individual conscience proclaims certainly against it. We are touching the fringe of one of the most vexed questions of canon law ; nevertheless it is possible to state a certain number of considerations which command the essential agreement of all writers. Our simplest course is to summarise the main conclusions on the subject given by Sylvester Prierias, the indefatigable encyclopædist who, at the very beginning of the modern era, gathered together all that the Middle Ages had written on law and ethics into a single exhaustive volume.[1] This account may be amplified from the fuller treatment of the question by Suarez ;[2] and a parallel discussion of Jeremy Taylor's will serve to show that the greatest of Anglican moralists is on this subject in entire agreement with the Schoolman and the Jesuit.

We are concerned, let us remember, with principles which not merely enable custom legitimately to introduce and to explain law, but also legitimately to abrogate it. Sylvester reduces the tests of legitimate custom for these purposes to two—it must be ' reasonable ' and it must be ' prescribed.' As to its ' reasonableness,' he considers various possible definitions. Thus it has been suggested that custom is ' reasonable ' if the law does not impugn it, but rather upholds it. This, however, is unsatisfactory, because it

---

[1] *Summa Summarum Sylvestrina*, s.v. ' Consuetudo.'
[2] *de legg.*, lib. vii.

does not give any principle for deciding cases where there is a clash between custom and an apparently obsolete law. Again, it has been suggested that only a judge can decide when custom is legitimate ; but this too is inadequate, for two judges might very well disagree about the same custom. He therefore decides on the following : ' A custom is reasonable when it conforms to the purpose of the law, and this, in the case of canon law, is the felicity of the soul. . . . It must, therefore, be to the advantage of religion, discipline, and salvation ' (§ 2). With this may be compared Suarez's definition. After rejecting as too vague a suggestion by Azpilcueta (Navarrus) that a custom is rational ' if it is not opposed either directly or indirectly to divine or natural law,' he lays down that no custom can be considered rational if it is ' detrimental to the liberty of the Church, or provides licence or occasion for sin, or is dangerous to the common weal, etc., even though it be not contrary to the divine law.' [1]

The subject of ' prescription ' (§ 4) is too technical to be considered here. In essence it implies that no custom is legitimate unless it has secured undisturbed observance for a certain length of time ; but as to the length of time necessary for legitimate prescription, canonists have differed widely. Usually, also, it is held that a longer period is necessary for the legitimate prescription of a custom abrogating law, than of one merely introducing or interpreting law. In the Roman Church the question has been settled by the clear definition of the new Codex [2] that for the abrogation of ecclesiastical law a prescription of forty years is necessary ; for the abrogation of a law definitely forbidding future customs to the contrary, an ' immemorial time.' No custom, of course, can abrogate the natural or positive divine law,[3] at all events as far as their first principles are concerned (§ 14).

---

[1] *Op. cit.*, vii. 6.                    [2] Can. 27.
[3] Cp. *S.T.*, i. 2, q. 97, a. 3 ; q. 94, aa. 4, 5 ; q. 95, a. 2.

Further conditions are, however, necessary according to all authorities, and these also Sylvester notices. The custom must be introduced by individual acts (which, as Suarez points out,[1] include 'omissions') because it is 'by the repetition of visible acts that the interior purpose of the will and the intention of the reason are most clearly exhibited; for anything that is constantly repeated appears to have its cause in a deliberate purpose of reason' (§ 3). It follows from this that there must be evidence of a general intention to introduce the custom, 'on account of its general useful- ness,' as Suarez says, 'or to the honour of religion.' Suarez illustrates this by an example. The Christian normally sleeps between his last meal at night and his morning com- munion; but as there is no evidence here that the Christian conscience intended to introduce a custom of sleeping during the fasting period, it would be absurd to allege that such a sleep is an authoritative custom binding in conscience.[2] A difficult question, however, remains. What is to be said of customs introduced in ignorance or error as to the law? Do they abrogate it? Suarez himself, on the principle that no 'intention' against the law can be alleged in such cases, tends to deny that they induce legitimate custom: he admits, however, that other authorities take the opposite view.[3]

The custom must be general in the 'multitude' for whom it is to have the force of law (§ 5), or at least general and public enough to make it clear that the community as a whole has taken notice of it and deliberately tolerates it (§ 6). It must also have the knowledge and at all events the tacit consent of the ultimate legislative authority, whatever that may be (§ 7). Positive laws can of course abrogate existing customs, but even this is subject to limitations. The law must be accepted 'moribus utentium,' and if it falls into desuetude, the custom can revive, at all events if the legis- lative authority is aware of the fact and takes no steps (§ 12).

[1] loc. cit., c. 10.　　　[2] Ib. c. 14.　　　[3] Ib.

But a positive law does not abrogate the contrary custom of a particular locality or community, unless some provision directly or indirectly ordering such abrogation is inserted in the law.   On the other hand, a custom once condemned by law can only be legitimately re-introduced if new reasons in support can be adduced for it (§ 10).

Jeremy Taylor's discussion [1] is (as often) diffuse, but in substance his conclusions are identical with the mediæval view.   The conditions he recognises are as follows :  (1) The custom must be ' reasonable and fit for wise and sober persons ' ; [2] (2) ' of present observation ' ; (3) ' not against the law ' where the law is ' warm and refreshed and calls for obedience ' ;  (4) ' useful ' or ' to the good of the soul,' ' honourable to religion or a mystery ' (so he approves the customs that ' the consecration of bishops should be in public churches ;  < and > that the degree of doctor, because it is an honour, be not conferred sneakingly and in conventicles ') ;  (5) ' of long abode ' if not ' of an immemorial time.'

It must clearly be a matter of extreme difficulty to decide how far any given or alleged custom satisfies conditions such as these, and so becomes obligatory ; we can easily understand why the Roman Church should have set herself to substitute canon for custom as far as possible. Furthermore, it is only the individual who can decide for himself (using the advice of ' prudent men,' of course, as much as he will), the legitimacy, *for him,* of a given custom ; for the moment a custom is declared by authority

---

[1] *Duct. Dub.,* iii. 4, rule 15.   More technical Anglican discussions will be found in Ayliffe, *Parergon,* pp. 194–196 ; Gibson, *Codex,* tit. xxx, c. 5 (on 2 Edw. VI, c. 13).   There is a valuable summary of the whole question in E. C. Wood, *Regal Power of the Church,* pp. 78–84.

[2] Curiously enough it is on this ground that he dismisses as invalid the custom that infants, in danger of death, should be baptised by their nurses ; ' because it leaned upon a false and superstitious opinion ; they thought it better to invade the priest's office than to trust God with the souls.'

to be obligatory, it ceases to become custom and becomes law. Let it be supposed then that a Christian is seriously concerned as to whether a particular custom satisfies the tests of legitimacy in such a way as to oblige him to obedience, or alternatively to release him from some obligation of a particular law ; his conscience not having proclaimed definitely and certainly either for or against it. He will, of course, use every means in his power to come to a decision ; but what is he to do in the meantime ? Should he conform or not conform ?

The principle which seems to give most guidance in such cases is that of the old maxim (recognised by all canonists and moralists) : ' In dubio melior est conditio possidentis.' [1] Whatever ' holds the field ' of the man's life—law, custom, or non-observance—may, and (except in the last instance) should, be left in possession until conscience gives a certain ruling. A law at present observed should not be broken until the individual is conscientiously certain that it has been legitimately abrogated by custom. A custom in present observance should, in the same way, be observed until it is clear that it has been generally abrogated by law or by desuetude. A custom observed by a part of the community, or by other branches of the Christian Church, does not bind any individual until he is conscientiously convinced that it has obtained the force of law within his own communion ; though, in this case, common sense itself decrees that nothing need prevent his adopting the custom, if he wishes to do so, before he is convinced of its legitimate prescription, provided always that it is not in itself morally undesirable, or in contravention of existing law.

[1] *Corp. Jur. Can.*, c. 6, X. ii. 26, where it is called a principle of ' both divine and human law.'

## V

Principles such as these seem to cover most of the cases of perplexity which can arise in the matter of conformity, even in the present condition of uncertainty as to doctrine and morals obtaining in the Church of England—a condition, be it said, not necessarily to be adjudged undesirable or unwise. Where a principle of faith or morals is firmly held or firmly rejected by an individual with a certain conscience, he is in conscience bound so to believe and so to act. He would be false, otherwise, to the eternal Truth and the eternal Goodness of the God whom he worships. But on all other points, and at all other times—not least of all in the general education of his conscience—he must judge according to these or similar rules. Where a principle has been re-affirmed by competent authority as part of the rule of faith or moral law of the Church, within a period recent enough to make it impossible for a contrary custom to have obtained legitimate prescription, it has a final obligation in all cases except those of a certain conscience to the contrary. Where, again, it is so commonly observed, that no reasonable person could believe it to be abrogated by contrary custom, its obligation is the same. Where neither of these conditions obtains, and a man is doubtful as to the right course of action in a matter of conduct, or the truth in a matter of faith, whilst conscience (which includes, as always, the use of such powers of reason as God has given) utters an uncertain voice, a temporary yet valid decision can be reached, in full conformity with the historic practice of Christendom, along the lines suggested.

It is not to be supposed that one man in a thousand is capable of thinking out for himself, on principles such as these, the innumerable perplexities with which his religion is bound to confront him. But it is urgently necessary that the clergy, with whom still rests in private as in public the guidance of the individual conscience, should be in possession of such principles, and be influenced by them in their advice and exhortation. So it may be possible to avoid both the Scylla of allowing men unwarned to trifle lightly with grave and existing obligations, and equally the Charybdis of importing into teaching of an official or semi-official character obligations which do not really obtain in the present condition of the Church of England. In the meantime it is possible still to hold that the general toleration, in our communion, of beliefs and practices widely at variance one with another is in no way proof that the traditional principles of Christian authority have been set aside in favour of a merely modern and anarchical libertinism. The distinctive note of Anglicanism, as we have seen, is the preference of custom to law ; and this in itself is a legitimate variation of Catholic principle. But where custom, with all its degrees of uncertainty, rules the day ; and where (moreover) only the individual can decide what customs oblige and what do not ; divergences due to conscientious nonconformity are bound to occur, and that probably in large numbers. On the principles of moral theology concerning invincible ignorance, these divergences, however numerous they may be, are all capable of condonation as wholly conscientious and blameless. It may indeed be urged that the wide differences of thought and practice tolerated in the Anglican communion are evidence of as widespread an ' ignorance ' (or, as was said before, ' incredulity ' or ' stupidity ') among the members of that communion. But in so much as it is possible that in every case the ignorance may be ' invincible,' the differences in themselves cannot be attributed out of hand to either lawlessness or laxity ; they may be the very symptoms of refined conscientiousness.

One caution remains to be emphasised. It is often

M

urged against the Roman system of law that it involves and encourages the dangers of formalism. However that may be, it is certainly true that the supremacy of ' custom ' in Anglicanism makes the possibility of laxity very real. We must be sure that the ' ignorance ' which leads to divergences is genuinely ' invincible ' ; that conscience and not convenience dictates them. Whether the tests of conscientiousness quoted at an earlier stage [1] are adequate or not, they are at least stringent and wholesome. They might be added to : they could hardly be relaxed. Every member of the Church of England who welcomes the comparative freedom from the dominance of law which that communion offers him should at least be urged to apply these tests to his own conscience, whenever it suggests a course not conformable to the dominant law or customs of his Church. Only so can the Anglican system, which, by the specific experiment it has initiated within the legitimate bounds of true Catholicism, has once and for all avoided the dangers of a merely formal uniformity, avoid also the equal danger of a wholly disruptive laxity, and so prove its experiment to be not only legitimate, but in the end successful too.

[1] *Supra*, pp. 34–36. I have quoted elsewhere (*Some Principles of Moral Theology*, pp. 189, 190) more detailed and searching tests given by Jeremy Taylor.

# INDEX

'Saracens,' 20, 50
Satan, 20
Scotus, Duns ; Scotists, 36, 109
Scripture, contradictions, 65 ; in-
  fallibility, 105
Seneca, 78
Sens, Council of (A.D. 1140), 13
Seyssel, C. de (Archbishop), 90–93,
  94, 95, 96
Sibylla, Bartholomew, 88, 89
Signs, evidence of, 105
Simony, 20, 153
Sin, causes of, 28 ; capital, 54 ;
  formal and material, 7 ; mortal
  and venial, 4, 68, 69 ; original,
  64, 69 ; philosophic, 86 ; Abai-
  lard on, 7–10
Slater, T., 45
Sodom, 72
Soissons, Council of (A.D. 1121), 75
Sommervogel, C., 82, 86
Sophocles, 1
Soto, Dominic, 51, 65, 84, 85, 121
Spirit, gifts and fruits of, 57
Steganography, 90
Stillingfleet, Bishop, 147
Stoics, 2
Stölzle, R., 75
Stubbs, W. (Bishop), 149
Suarez, F., 3, 5, 6, 47, 102, 111 ; on
  custom, 146, 147, 156–157 ; faith,
  66, 71, 83, 84, 100, 123–128 ;
  ignorance, 60, 61 ; law, 140–142 ;
  salvation, 64, 72, 83, 84 ; sanc-
  tions, 152, 153
'Sufficiency,' test of, 52, 53, 123
Summa Summarum Sylvestrina, 50
Suppléances providentielles, 94
Syllabus (1864), 63, 84
Sylvester Prierias (Mozolinus), 50,
  155–158
Sylvius, F., 65
Symmachus, 89
Syro-Phœnician woman, 90, 91

TANQUEREY, A., 36, 63, 109, 111,
  130, 131, 133, 148
Tardif, A., 148

Taylor, J. (Bishop), 5, 35, 36, 42,
  45, 61, 142, 146, 152, 158, 162
Tertullian, 2, 65, 72, 100, 146
Theodore of Mopsuestia, 74
Theodoric, 89
Thomas of Ely, 11
Thucydides, 1
Tostado, A. (Bishop), 88
Trent, Council of (A.D. 1545–1563),
  72, 79, 85, 142
Trinity, see Faith, explicit and
  implicit
Tritheim, J., 88–90, 93, 95, 96, 97

UNIVERSALISM, 72–78

VACANT, A., 130 ; see also Harent
Valentinian, 6
Vasquez, Gabriel, 35, 59, 123
Vatican Council (A.D. 1870), 103,
  108, 111–112
Vega, Andreas, 65, 67, 72, 76, 78–81,
  83, 84, 94, 97
Victoria, Francis à, 50–53, 59, 70,
  87, 89, 123
Virtues, 57 ; theological, 115–118
'Vision,' 99
Vives, Ludovic, 77
von Hügel, Baron F., 60
voto, in, faith, baptism, 71, 83

WAKEMAN, H. O., 149
Waldenses, 90
Walker, T. A., 51
Wall, W., 78
War, 'just,' 51
Werner, K., 87
Wilkins, D., 76
Will, sinful, 6
William of Corvo, 89
William of Paris, 67
William of St. Thierry, 13
Wood, E. C., 140, 158
Wycliffe, J., 76

ZELLER, E., 1
Zwingli, U., 78

Printed in England at THE BALLANTYNE PRESS
SPOTTISWOODE, BALLANTYNE & CO. LTD.
Colchester, London & Eton